FORGOTTEN HAUNTINGS OF NORTHEAST OHIO

FORGOTTEN HAUNTINGS OF NORTHEAST OHIO

WILLIAM G. KREJCI

Haunted America

Published by Haunted America
A division of The History Press
An imprint of Arcadia Publishing
Charleston, SC
www.historypress.com

First published 2025

Manufactured in the United States

ISBN 9781467170475
Hardcover ISBN 9781540299826

Library of Congress Control Number: 2025940392

CONTENTS

PREFACE

In 2018, I started to compile a number of newspaper articles and reports on paranormal and ghostly activity that hadn't been covered in over a century. I've since named this work the Forgotten Hauntings Project. It all began while I was doing the research for *Ghosts and Legends of Northern Ohio*, which was released by The History Press in 2019. That book tackled the best known ghostly legends from the area and investigated their origins in an attempt to set the record straight on some of our favorite tall tales—with a paranormal twist. Here and there, I stumbled upon a story that I'd never come across before. In fact, when I looked further into these, I discovered that no one had. There was no evidence, whatsoever, that they had been covered in any way, shape or form since they were first reported on more than one hundred years ago. Thus, the Forgotten Hauntings Project was born.

As I unearthed more and more of these tales, I realized that I had enough to organize my findings and put them into a book. I was rather astonished when I realized how many stories I had actually accumulated. It turned out that I had enough to write not one but at least five books on the subject. Being a Clevelander, I decided to start with what I knew best, and that was home. So, 2023's *Lost Ghost Stories of Cleveland* was released.

With the success of that book, I knew I had to write another, only this time, I would cover the entirety of Northern Ohio. Unfortunately, again, I had too many stories and had to narrow that book's scope down to Northeast Ohio. Since writing that last book, I've discovered a few more tales from

Cuyahoga County that I had somehow overlooked before. This was a perfect opportunity for me to get those out there.

But as I said, I had enough to write at least five books. As far as the rest of the stories go, I'll be playing it close to the vest for the time being.

As has been done in the past, I've included GPS coordinates at the start of the chapter. These should aid the reader in pinpointing the precise locations of these storied hauntings. In some cases, the buildings are still standing. In other cases, sadly, they have been lost to time.

One last thing that I would like to add: in conducting the research for this book, I ended up with a few stories whose exact locations couldn't quite be pinpointed. Rather than excluding them from this work, I thought it was better to present them, along with the research and the subsequent dead end. In doing this, I cordially invite you, the reader, to take a crack at solving these mysteries for yourself. You may prove be a better detective than you thought.

I will say this: once you get started, it's hard to stop.

ACKNOWLEDGEMENTS

I would like to extend a special thanks to the following, without whose assistance and guidance, this book would not have been possible. Firstly, I wish to thank my parents, George and Mary Krejci; my siblings, Tom Krejci and Jenn Dobbins; as well as their spouses, Emma and Burt. I also want to thank the rest of my family and all of my friends for their unending encouragement and support. I also wish to extend thanks to Joe Gartrell, Ashley Hill, Anna Burrous, the photo, editorial and marketing teams and the entire staff at The History Press. A huge debt of gratitude also goes out to Ryan McCarbery and Christina Johnson for accompanying me on so many amazing adventures; to Geoff Hanks, who I was truly blessed to know and whose friendship was one absolutely amazing adventure; to Gavin Esposito, whose enthusiasm for history knows no bounds. Thanks also goes out to the following for their priceless contributions to this work: Lesley Patterson; Mark Tidrick, Brian Meggitt and the Cleveland Public Library Photograph Collection; Ann Sindelar, Liz Konopka and the Western Reserve Historical Society Library; the Library of Congress; Rebecca Larson-Troyer and the Akron-Summit County Public Library; Elizabeth A. Piwkowski and the Michael Schwartz Library Special Collections at Cleveland State University; Johanna Wilkes, Joan Demirjian and the *Chagrin Valley Times*; Ken Grossi and the Oberlin College Archives; Brandon Massullo; Jeffrey L. Monseau and Springfield College; Ashley Miller; Debbie Hensley, the Thornton family and the Portage Lakes Historical Society; Judith G. Cetina and the Cuyahoga County Archives; Charles Cassady; Beth A. Richards and Chuck L. Gove; Tracie Pickett, Vic Fleisher and the University of Akron Archives and Special Collections; Mark Holland and the McKinley Presidential Library and Museum; Medina County District Library and the Sharon Township Heritage Society; the Richland County Auditor's Office; the Lorain County Auditor's Office; the Ashtabula County Auditor's Office; and Carrie Wimer and the Ashtabula County District Library.

1

Daniel Harmon Fargo's Tenant House

The last tenant held out for a month, but at last he gave up like the rest, and cleared out, although he had done the place up thoroughly, and must have been pounds out of the pocket by the transaction.
—The Ghost of Jerry Bundler, *by W.W. Jacobs and Charles Rock*

Our volume of forgotten ghostly tales begins with a mystery. It was on November 19, 1859, that the *Ashtabula Weekly Telegraph* broke the story of a haunted house out in Ashtabula's East Village neighborhood, just across the river from town. "Ghosts Around," begins the article. It goes on to explain that some within the East Village, for days and nights past, had been a little "exercised" by the presence, or supposed presence, of ghosts or superhuman agencies in their midst. The scene of the haunting in question was a tenant house that belonged to the esteemed D.H. Fargo.

Daniel Harmon Fargo was born in Ashtabula on August 29, 1819, to parents Jason and Clarissa Harmon Fargo. His father had come to Ohio from Berkshire County, Massachusetts, and purchased a farm that comprised 156 acres. Jason's wife, Clarissa, hailed from that same county in Massachusetts. During the first years of the 1820s, Jason and Clarissa Fargo built a fine brick house, which still stands. Their farm of 156 acres has since been replaced by a neighborhood.

By the late 1850s, at which time the story of the haunting was unfolding, Jason and Clarissa's son, Daniel, had accumulated a fair amount of land as well and was regarded as a pillar of the community. It would stand to reason

A present-day view of the Fargo House, which stands at 4321 State Road in Ashtabula. *Photo courtesy of the Ashtabula County Auditor's Office.*

that the neighbors, by and large, would be surprised by a claim that a tenant house belonging to such a highly regarded individual would be haunted.

A family named Hammond occupied the house at the time. It was their claim that they had been much terrified by sounds and sights of an unearthly character. Further reports claimed rattling and unexplained opening and slamming of doors, even after every precaution to secure them had been taken. The fears of the Hammond family spread, and the stories regarding the tenant house circulated. This all led to action. A number of men within the community decided to find out the source of the haunting and even chose to spend the night within the haunted house.

One of these men, after spending a night, explained to a reporter that either the ghosts had prudently kept themselves out of the way or he simply lacked the vividness of imagination to catch any trace of them. It was explained that the premises had been, for some time, quietly reported as an abode of spirits and that these whispered rumors, which reached the ears of the occupants, were the principal cause of exciting their minds.

The reader will notice that, at the top of this story, the GPS coordinates for the location of Daniel Harmon Fargo's tenant house are missing. The secret of its location is the true mystery here. A landownership map from

A view of East Village looking east from State Road. *From* A History of Ashtabula County, Ohio, *1924*.

1856 exists; however, the top portion of this map, where Ashtabula would be found, is missing. If the missing portion of this map could be located, so, too, might the secret location of this storied abode. A map from 1874 does exist, and it clearly shows a fifty-five acre tract that belonged to D.H. Fargo, but no house is indicated. Immediately to the north sits the massive farm of Jason Fargo, Daniel's father, but at the time of this map's printing, Jason Fargo had been deceased for thirteen years. On that land, two structures are marked. The lower one is marked "Res.," being the fine brick residence that Jason Fargo built in the early 1820s. Could the structure indicated above "Res." be the reputed haunted house? If so, it would have sat near the present-day northwest corner of the intersection of State Road and East 42nd Street.

Based on the conclusion of the article that reported this haunting, it appears that a good number of those who resided in Ashtabula's East Village had taken a set against the *Weekly Telegraph*, its editor in particular. The article's author took this opportunity to hurl an insult at that community's residents by stating, "What object the Devil could have in visiting East Village, is more than we can imagine. That he has friends there, is not altogether improbable, but that they are such novices as to require his presence and supervision, we can scarcely believe."

2

OHIO CITY'S WHITMAN STREET HAUNTING

Much as she dreaded it, she must spend the night alone in that big bedroom—the haunted bedroom where the last of the Peveril's died.
—The Third Time, *by Grant Allen*

"Another Bugaboo!"

So announces a headline from the *Cleveland Plain Dealer*, dated Friday, June 4, 1869—a full ten years after the report of the haunting of Daniel Harmon Fargo's tenant house in Ashtabula. The article fails to explain what the previous bugaboo was.

This newly discovered haunting was reported in Cleveland's Ohio City neighborhood, but again, a mystery exists, as the newspaper fails to give an exact location of the home; not even the name of the tenant is revealed. The article shares only that the otherworldly activity was witnessed by a woman who resided on Whitman Street between Kentucky and Taylor Streets.

The following day, greater details in this case were revealed. It was claimed by the occupant that every night, the windows, doors, shutters and even the walls of the house itself shook continually, as though some heavy object was being constantly thrown against the building or as if the house was experiencing some form of an earthquake. The phenomenon was, of course, attributed to a ghostly presence, though no such entity had been witnessed previously at that address.

It was said that the occupant was a lady of more than ordinary nerve who announced her intention of remaining there, ghost or no ghost, until

A present-day view of Whitman Avenue in Ohio City. *Photo by William G. Krejci.*

the cause of the disturbances could be ascertained. As word of the matter circulated throughout the neighborhood, many people began to descend on the residence to witness the goings-on firsthand. Of course, a variety of opinions regarding the source of the issue were expressed, but none seemed plausible and no solution to the matter could be determined. Until another satisfactory answer could be had, most simply accepted the concept that troubled spirits were the source of the commotion.

Curiously, that first week of June 1869 turned out to be quite an exciting time for little Whitman Street. On June 1, a cow that belonged to one George Delling of nearby 39 Chatham Street got loose and subsequently attacked a boy at the corner of Whitman and Kentucky Streets. A large crowd gathered to lend assistance, and it was suspected by many that the cow was mad. An officer named Thompson arrived at the scene and sent word to the owner to collect his cow or it would be destroyed. The owner never arrived, and the officer found himself with no other option but to kill the animal.

While this story is not paranormal in nature, it's just unfortunate all around. The location of that last incident is at least revealed, while the site of the Whitman Street haunting remains a mystery. If anyone should go looking for this house, it should be noted that Kentucky Street is now West 38th Street. Taylor Street now carries the designation West 45th Street. Curiously, Whitman Street never extended that far west and terminated at Harbor Street, presently West 44th Street, which significantly narrows the search parameters.

3

The Ghostly Grocer

41.506069, -81.686782

How stealthily the gray light comes! How ghost-like the white mist looks creeping along the ground, or wreathing into phantom-shapes among the bare, black boughs of trees! How barren and bereft of all beauty the earth seems!
—Morton House, *by Christian Reid*

On July 23, 1870, the *Cleveland Leader* broke the story of a strange case that was unfolding in Cleveland involving a widow, a medium and a recently deceased grocer.

A grocery merchant, whom the newspaper designates as "Mr. W.," passed away and was mourned as forever lost to his family and friends. As time passed, his bereaved family did the best they could with their limited means to gain a livelihood, following the business of the dead husband and father.

The author of the article refuses to reveal the late grocer's true name but suggests that it can easily be learned by asking any business owner on Saint Clair Street between Erie and Dodge Streets. The only other thing related was that both the grocer and his wife were originally from Germany.

Around mid-July 1870, the deceased grocer's wife became acquainted with a spiritual medium, and while visiting this medium at her home one night, the widow jokingly asked her to show her some sign of her late husband. At this, the room was suddenly filled with a pale gray light, and a moment later, the form of the woman's departed husband stood before her. He appeared just as she'd remembered him when she'd last seen him. He said not a word but simply stood there, glaring at the women.

After the spirit departed, the grocer's widow, being too afraid to go home, asked the medium if she might stay the night at her place, to which the medium agreed. Soon after, the two retired for the night.

All was quiet in the medium's house until around one o'clock in the morning, at which time, the medium was awakened by the sight of her room being filled with a brilliant light. Looking around the room, she saw her friend, the grocer's widow, sitting up in a chair with her clothing being placed on her by some unseen force, as if by magic. In no time at all, the woman was dressed from head to toe and quietly departed the medium's house. Satisfied that it was all the work of the spirit of the late grocery merchant, who must have had a higher purpose for doing this, the medium returned to bed and slept until her husband, a rolling mill employee, returned home from work, at which time she related to him the story of what had occurred.

The following day, the medium paid a visit to her friend to learn about what happened after she left. The widow explained that she really knew nothing of it, except that the next thing she was aware of, she was at the bedside of her late husband's mother, who was suddenly stricken with an attack of illness.

The widow of the late grocer was still somewhat skeptical, in spite of the visitation of her husband's spirit the previous night. In reply, the medium invited the widow to take a walk with her that evening.

As evening fell, the two women met up and went for a stroll, the result of which astonished them both. While quietly walking along, the grocer's widow suddenly grasped her companion's arm and asked in a whisper, "Do you see him?"

"Certainly," replied the medium. "He has been behind us for a square."

Realizing that it was again the spirit of her late husband, the frightened widow hugged her friend tighter, and the two briskly made their way back to the medium's house.

After that night, the shadowy presence of the ghostly grocer, the widow contended, constantly haunted her. It strained her nerves to their limit, and she constantly spoke into the air, as if in conversation with some unseen but terrible power. The writer of the article explained that the story was shared as it was related but doesn't vouch for its truth—although they do vouch for the sincerity of those involved and those who related the tale.

While the names of the grocer, his wife, the medium and all the others involved in this story were withheld, one too many clues were volunteered. After spending countless nights looking over city directories,

An advertisement for C. Smith. *From* The Cleveland City Directory, *1867*.

advertisements, newspaper articles and census and death records, the identity of Mr. W. was finally gleaned, as there was only one person who fit all the criteria perfectly.

Christian Smith, whose surname appears in some records as "Schmidt," was born in Germany in 1832. He immigrated to the United States and settled in Cleveland, where, in April 1856, he was married to Mary E. Shieley, who also hailed from Germany. The two raised at least five children. During the Civil War, Christian Smith served in the 104th Ohio Infantry, and upon being discharged, he returned to Cleveland, where he established a grocery firm at 341 Saint Clair Street. This business, also the family residence, sat on the northwest corner at Brownell Street, later called Canfield Street and now called East 13th Street. As the author of the article hints, this location is perfectly situated between Erie and Dodge Streets, today called East 9th Street and East 17th Street, respectively.

Christian Smith passed away from typhoid fever on May 31, 1870, at the age of thirty-eight. Originally interred in the city vaults at Erie Street Cemetery, his remains were transferred to Woodland Cemetery, where he was laid to rest on June 9 in section 5, lot 5. Less than a year later, that same lot received another burial. A nineteen-year-old man, also named Christian Smith, was laid to rest beside the late grocer. Smith had no children of this age and name, so it's possible the young man may have been a nephew or some other close relative.

Christian Smith's monument at section 5, lot 5, grave 2 in Cleveland's Woodland Cemetery. *Photo by William G. Krejci.*

Today, the site of Christian Smith's grocery and home, where he was said to haunt his grieving wife, is a parking lot on the northwest corner of Saint Clair Avenue and East 13th Street.

4
Philander Chandler's Spirited Windows

41.080738, -81.769735

Then at the window came a noise—
They look, and see a beckoning hand,
And their dead father, looking in,
In his black preacher's cassock stand.
—*"The Preacher's Family," by Heinrich Heine*

"The spirits at Sharon, Medina County, are engaged in painting, or forming portraits on window panes, similar to those which have been witnessed in several other places, and are creating considerable excitement in that neighborhood."

So begins an article that appeared in Ravenna's *Democratic Press* on October 26, 1871. According to the story, these manifestations were showing up at quite a few houses in the area, but nowhere more so than at the beautiful home of Philander Chandler.

Philander Chandler was born on December 20, 1828, in Unadilla, Otsego County, New York, to parents Silas and Nancy Farnsworth Chandler. He came to Ohio with his family in 1831, first residing in Norton, but six months later, the Chandlers settled in Sharon Township. Philander attended school at Oberlin College, where he received a classical education. He continued his education at Medina College, where he graduated with a law degree, and was later admitted to the bar.

Philander Chandler got swept up in the gold rush fever of 1849 and headed out to California with his brother, Henry, around 1850. He remained there for five years, working primarily as a drover. Still, he must have accumulated a fair degree of wealth. Two years into his stint in California, he sent money home to Sharon and purchased a farm of 233 acres. Upon his return in 1855, he built a fine home on lot 62 in Sharon Township. In 1858, Philander Chandler was married to Susan C. Cox and, with her, raised four children.

As for the mysterious happenings at the Chandler home in 1871, the newspaper reported that these events were witnessed firsthand by the editor of the *Wadsworth Enterprise*. In his account, the editor noted that, when inspecting the windows at the Chandler house, he and the others who had gathered with him observed what appeared to be a human face in a pane of an upper window. Some of those present pointed out that there was something of a resemblance between this image and the likeness of Abraham Lincoln. Others saw similarities to one Professor Peck of Oberlin. The image in question had been discovered a week earlier and was starting to fade a little.

Other panes around the house, nearly twenty in all, showed a variety of different images, including faces, landscapes, vines, cities—and yet some were quite irregular and showed no definite image but were composed of brilliantly colorful lines. When viewing these images from inside the home, no trace could be detected, yet when standing outside and away from the house, a distance of 6 to 8 rods, that being approximately 100 to 130 feet, the incredible images could plainly be seen. All efforts to remove the images by washing had proven unsuccessful.

Of course, a number of theories were put forth about the cause of the ghostly images. Some had suggested that it was a natural force at work, in a photographic form, while others believed it to be a trick of the heat and cold applied to the different sides of the glass under shaded conditions. The windows in question were sometimes shuttered during the summer months to deflect the intensity of the sun. The editor was quite certain that these weren't the result of human hands, but he was also skeptical of a supernatural source.

As previously mentioned, Philander Chandler's house wasn't the only residence in the vicinity that exhibited this otherworldly phenomenon. It was noted that similar images also appeared at the house of a neighbor, Joseph Fixler, and the home of Philander Chandler's brother, Henry Z. Chandler. The latter of these displayed a very fine landscape view.

It should also be noted that the house occupied by Henry Z. Chandler gained notoriety of its own in later years, as it was Sharon Township's famous haunted house. That residence was built in 1850 by Edward Barber

The residence of Philander Chandler on Fixler Road in Sharon Township. *From* Combination Atlas Map of Medina County, Ohio, *1874.*

Bentley. A *Plain Dealer* article, dated September 5, 1915, shared the story of the haunted mansion at Sharon, which was said to be visited by the ghost of a young woman who died in the home over half a century earlier. The storyteller relating the tale, Reverend Joshua Crawford of the Sharon Center Methodist Church, chose to change the names of the families involved in the account, using instead the surnames "Bader" for the central family of the story and "Warrett" for a rival family who lived across the road. I've taken the liberty of giving the families their original names, those respectively being Bentley and Warner. The story, in short, goes like this:

Two well-to-do families settled in southwest Sharon Township, and there, each built very pretentious homes, one right across the road from the other. These two families were very competitive in their community and always tried to outdo the other.

In time, it was learned that the Bentleys daughter Lottie was a very gifted spiritual medium. The family would host regular séances in their home, which greatly incensed the Warners. One foggy, moonless night, the Warner house mysteriously caught fire, and the alarm was sent out. None worked harder to extinguish the flames than Mr. Bentley. Still, the house was in absolute ruin, and rather than rebuild, the Warners packed up and moved west. Lottie Bentley held a séance and, through knowledge gained from spirits on the other side, claimed that a deceased former hired hand of the Warners had maliciously caused a pile of rags in a closet to ignite. Still, some believed that Lottie may have known more than what she was sharing.

Not long after the fire, Lottie Bentley fell ill and discontinued her séances. As she lay on her deathbed, she asked her mother to bring her some tea. Her mother prepared tea and toast and brought it to her. Lottie then seemed to want to talk about the fire at the Warners' house, but her father prevented her from doing so. Later that night, just around the time that Lottie passed away, her mother claimed she witnessed the headless apparition of a woman bent over the kitchen stove, making tea and toast. The specter told Mrs. Bentley that she would have to do this once a week for the rest of her days.

Shortly before her passing, Lottie made a request of her parents. It was her wish that she not be buried at the local graveyard; rather, she wanted to be laid to rest as close to the kitchen door as possible so that she could be near her parents and able to easily visit them from time to time. This request was granted, and Lottie was buried in a grave near the fence, close to the house.

About a week later, Lottie's voice was heard calling to her mother, asking her to bring her some tea and something to eat. Though the girl was dead, her mother obliged. This went on every week for a number of years until, at last, the mother also passed. Later tenants reported heavy trampling sounds in the sitting room, the sound of chains rattling down the stairs and even being grabbed by what they believed was the ghost of Lottie Bentley. Lottie's grave was ultimately exhumed and reinterred at Sharon Center Cemetery, where she now takes her repose.

Many years later, the house was owned by a man named John Potter Beech, who didn't really believe in ghosts. The year following his death in 1920, the "haunted house" was sold to a real estate firm in Wadsworth.

This story, as well as a story regarding John Beech's time at the Bentley house, is excellently related in greater detail in the book *Haunted Medina County, Ohio*, by Brandon Massullo. These stories can be found in chapter 15, "The Farmer Who Could Dodge Bullets," and chapter 16, "The Medium Buried Under the Kitchen Door." Though these stories appear in two separate chapters, both, it turns out, took place in the same house. Brandon Massullo expertly shares those stories, and little more can be added to them.

Though greatly modified over the years, having once been a sixteen-room mansion, the Bentley house was reduced in size and still stands at 2057 Fixler Road.

Regarding the home of Philander Chandler, which drew such attention for the ghostly images on its windows in 1871, the house and farm were sold to Charles E. Swigart around 1880. At this time, Chandler moved to Pittsfield, Michigan, where he was engaged in the hotel trade. He died there on March 1, 1888, and was buried in Ann Arbor.

During the first half of the twentieth century, the Philander Chandler house was torn down. A modern house was built on the site in 1939, and it still stands today.

5

THE PEFFERS HOUSE

41.240703, -80.808835

No mortal knows it but myself, and I see it coming upon me with slow, but unconquerable power. Oh, God—dreadful Spirit—spare me!
—The Evil Guest, *by Joseph Sheridan Le Fanu*

The city of Warren was founded in 1798. Two years later, Trumbull County was established, and it encompassed the entire Connecticut Western Reserve, this being most of Northeast Ohio. It was decided that Warren, not Cleveland, should serve as the county seat. Over the years, of course, sections of Trumbull County were broken off, and new counties were established from these sections. Although it's now a much smaller county than it was at its establishment, Warren remains the county seat of Trumbull.

Warren, in time, also became the home of Sylvester Wesley Peffers. Born in 1843 and raised in Lawrence County, Pennsylvania, this young man found himself in Warren at the start of the U.S. Civil War, and in 1862, he enlisted as a private in Company E of the 54th Ohio Volunteer Infantry. Sylvester Peffers was captured by Confederate troops in early 1865 and was held as a prisoner of war in Lynch Creek, South Carolina. After his release and the conclusion of the war, he returned to Warren, moved into a house on Market Street and followed the occupation of a carpenter. On January 3, 1867, he was married to Sarah A. Long. Together, they raised five daughters.

In the early 1870s, Sylvester and Sarah moved their family into a house on the north end of Chestnut Street, where in 1875, a tale of a haunting emerged. On October 2 that year, the story broke that the Peffers' home on Chestnut Street was haunted, and that the family could not be induced to stay in the house overnight.

Crowds of people descended on the Pefferses' house at night in hopes of catching a glimpse of the ghost. Quite a few claimed they saw it, and what they described was a blue mist that would move all about the house. It was mostly witnessed at night between the hours of nine o'clock and midnight.

Mr. Peffers related that the first time he saw the ghost, it came right up to his side. He attempted to reach for it, but it vanished without a trace. He further went on to explain that there was a door between his bedroom and the sitting room that, when closed, was very difficult to open. He asserted that he closed the door three different nights, and when he woke the following mornings, the door was open.

The citizens of Warren were convinced that it was no hoax.

The Pefferses' house was located on the east side of present-day Chestnut Avenue, just south of its intersection with Woodland Street, the Pefferses having owned lots 7 and 8 on Chestnut Avenue. Those lots ultimately contained three houses, though only the two that occupy the southern

This empty lot on Chestnut Avenue marks the former site of the Peffers House in Warren. *Photo by William G. Krejci.*

portion of that land are still standing. Even at that, those houses were built around 1920. This could only mean that the northernmost house, the one that no longer stands, was that of the Pefferses.

Causing some confusion in researching this story, the report incorrectly claimed the haunted house was the home of "I.W. Peffers," but no such person existed, only S.W. Peffers. It was also noticed that, in many cases, the first letter of his first name very much resembled the letter I when written down.

Sylvester and Sarah Peffers sold their Chestnut Street property on January 23, 1880, to Sarah Peffers's brother, Allan H. Long, and moved back to Market Street.

6

The Haunted House on West Tuscarawas Street

40.799450, -81.381484

Can storied urn or animated bust
Back to its mansion call the fleeting breath?
Can Honour's voice provoke the silent dust,
Or Flatt'ry soothe the dull cold ear of Death?
—*"Elegy Written in a Country Churchyard," by Thomas Gray*

Born on December 23, 1784, in Washington County, New York, Roswell Marsh Mason took up the occupation of an attorney and, around 1810, settled in Canton, then still a small village. It was there that he purchased ten acres immediately west of town from a man named Wells and proceeded to build "a large and convenient" two-story frame house on what is now West Tuscarawas Street. The house had a kitchen, while the property also boasted a large barn and well with a good pump and good water. In all, the property was valued at $1,720.

After a few years, Mason relocated to Warren to continue in his pursuits as a lawyer. He owed debts in Canton, and to satisfy these, he put his former home up for auction. It took about four years, but finally, in 1821, a buyer was found. Still, according to those who would recall the house in an account that appeared in *A History of Stark County, 1881*, the former home of Roswell M. Mason sat empty for a number of years, which gave it a very forlorn appearance. The creaking doors and windows soon gave it the reputation of being haunted. In time, a family named Burchfield took possession of the house but moved out a short time after, having been frightened away by

The Samuel Lahm House at 810 West Tuscarawas Street in Canton. *Photo courtesy of the McKinley Presidential Library & Museum (Canton, OH).*

A present-day view of 810 West Tuscarawas Street in Canton reveals it's now a parking lot. *Photo by William G. Krejci.*

uncanny noises, mostly at night and quite often exactly at midnight, when it was believed that ghosts most liked to wander.

Around that time, a man named Jerry Lind was engaged in trapping muskrats along nearby West Creek. He found the ghosts that haunted the old Mason house to be more provoking than frightening. According to Lind, the ghosts would constantly snatch the hat off his head as he passed the old house while going to or from his traps before daybreak. He claimed that he never saw anyone or anything, but he always claimed that he could never keep his hat on his head when passing that place.

Eventually, the Mason house was purchased by one Reverend James Morrow, who fixed up the dilapidated structure by making general repairs and adding some paint. This, many believed, drove off the evil spirits that dwelt there—or at least robbed the place of its haunted appearance.

Around 1850, the property was purchased by pioneer settler and lawyer and later U.S. Congressman Samuel Lahm. Shortly after, the house was demolished to make way for a grand mansion, which stood for a number of years at 810 West Tuscarawas Street. Though spooky in appearance, the home never had rumors of a haunting emerge. Today, the site is the parking lot immediately to the west of 800 West Tuscarawas Street.

7
Haunted House for Rent

41.509007, -81.684060

"I can assure you," said I, "that it will take a very tangible ghost to frighten me."
And I stood up before the fire with my glass in my hand.
"It's your own choosing," said the man with the withered arm,
and glanced at me askance.
—The Red Room, *by H.G. Wells*

Clinton Park, which once graced the city of Cleveland between present-day East 16th Street and East 18th Street on the north side of Lakeside Avenue, was described in the *Cleveland City Directory* for 1837 thus:

> *Situated half a mile from the court-house on the bank of Lake Erie—which although a wilderness of unsightly stumps and girdled trees two years ago, is already encircled with some suburban villas embosomed in gardens of the most picturesque beauty. The Park itself is about thirty rods in length and occupies the space between Wilson Street and Lake Street. It is intended to be laid out in the landscape style of gardening, comprising lawns, shrubbery, ornamental trees and flowers, which with the Mineral Spring adjacent, will be open to the public.*

Who would have imagined that one of those suburban villas would one day be regarded as a haunted house? So claimed an article from the *Cleveland Leader*, dated August 29, 1883. The article explained that a splendid opportunity awaited the man who was not afraid of ghosts to distinguish himself and, at the same time, add to his store of worldly riches. On Lake Street, near Clinton Park, stood a house, which the article claimed had been unoccupied for the greater part of the last few years. No one lived in the house for very long, and it was widely whispered among the neighbors that the house was infested with ghosts. A past resident confirmed these rumors, stating that mysterious sounds, such as rapping, pounding and scratching noises, could be heard at all hours, convincing them that the house was, in fact, under the influence of supernatural agencies.

One recent tenant was not superstitious but claimed that his wife would hear noises almost every night. He claimed he would have gladly stayed in the home, but his wife wouldn't have it, thus they moved out. The then-current owner, who now found it nearly impossible to rent out the house, wished to confirm or debunk the ghostly rumors attached to the house. At this, he offered it rent-free to any brave soul who would live there for six months. He was also willing to pay twenty-five dollars to anyone who had courage enough to spend an entire night in the house. Obviously, this article created quite a stir throughout the neighborhood.

The following evening, a small crowd of a little more than a dozen people gathered in front of an empty brick house on Lake Street, about a half a block west of Clinton Park, that bore a sign out front that read "For Rent." A few shared stories and suspicions on the house's possible violent past and what could be the cause of its haunting. One man suggested that they go inside and dig up the cellar floor, implying that there may be a skeleton buried beneath it.

A woman in the crowd related how, many years ago, two couples moved into the house but always kept the blinds closed. It was believed that they hosted late-night card parties, as crowds of well-dressed people were seen visiting the house regularly, with loud commotions coming from behind the drawn windows. A neighbor named Bill Hicks witnessed two large men walk in one night, immediately after which all of the lights inside were put out. The following morning, two trunks were removed from the house and loaded onto a train. A short time later, the two men came out of the house and departed Cleveland, but their wives were never seen to leave the premises.

Another family moved in afterward but soon moved out. It was said that screams were heard coming from the parlor, and a servant girl witnessed a ghostly woman in white running up the stairs past her, clutching at her breast, which was covered in blood. As the woman outside the house concluded her story to the assembled crowd, a boy who was hiding behind a fence across

THE WRONG HOUSE.

The Spook Hunters Not on the Right Track.

How a Crowd of Curious People Have Rendered Themselves Obnoxious.

Left: A headline declares that people who hoped to get a glimpse of the ghost assembled at "The Wrong House." *From the* Cleveland Leader, *August 31, 1883.*

Opposite, top: A view of Clinton Park on Lake Avenue while it was being used as a military camp during World War I. *Photo courtesy of the Western Reserve Historical Society.*

Opposite, bottom: A present-day view of the site of the house that formerly sat at 340 Lake Street. *Photo by William G. Krejci.*

the street threw a rock at the house, smashing out a window. At this, the crowd departed the scene.

The *Leader*, reporting on the gathering that night, explained that the crowd had, in fact, congregated at the wrong house. The haunted house in question was not a brick house, as those people had believed; rather, it was a wooden frame house. Furthermore, the haunted house had already been rented out. The *Plain Dealer*, which was now also covering the story, confirmed that the brick house, its given address being 293 Lake Street, was in fact the wrong house. The problem is that there was no house with an address of 293 Lake Street. The *Leader* set the record straight the next day and explained that the brick house that was suspected by the crowd of being the haunted house was located at 291 Lake Street.

Two days after the initial offer to let the house rent-free to a brave tenant was published, the *Leader* ran a statement from the owner of the brick house at 291 Lake Street, who shared his grievances about what had been done to his property. It seems that the crowd did worse than just throw a rock and break a window. Many people trampled the lawn, and some even went as far as to break into the house. None, it seems, were successful in digging up the cellar floor. Furthermore, the owner claimed that his house was never haunted.

So, if the haunted house was not located at 291 Lake Street, where was it?

After conducting a thorough search through countless newspaper advertisements, the only house listed as being for rent at that time that stood anywhere close to Clinton Park was the frame house that stood at 340 Lake Street, near the southeast corner of what was then Dodge and Lake Streets, now, respectively, East 17th Street and Lakeside Avenue. Not only was it located near Clinton Park, but more specifically, it also sat across the street

from it. Advertisements for the house share that it had "gas, bathrooms, and everything convenient." The house was occupied in 1874 by Alexander J. McCrea of James McCrea and Company, Beef and Pork Packers. Two years later, residency of the home was taken up by A.E. Dehler, who ran a saloon at 17 Frankfurt Street.

In 1886, the address was changed to 576 Lake Street, and in 1906, the address became 1708 Lakeside Avenue. The house was occupied until around 1918. It then sat derelict for the next ten years and was ultimately torn down. Currently, the site is occupied by The Illuminating Company's Hamilton Substation at 1245 East 17th Street.

The Dehler family, who moved into that house in 1876, continued to occupy the house until shortly before it went up for rent in 1883. This contradicts the idea that the haunted house had been largely unoccupied over the few years prior to the first article's publication. So, the real haunted house may be a different house altogether, one that was never advertised in the newspapers. Perhaps a reader would be willing to take a crack at this one to see if they can discover the actual address of the haunted house that went up for rent on Lake Street in 1883.

8
The Hazelton Saloon

He often heard terrible sounds—a mixture of the clangour of the trumpet and the howl of the wolf; he heard how at night time there was a soft moving about in the billiard-hall; how the balls rattled; small bells were rung, and so on.
—The H——— Family, *by Fredrika Bremer*

Thursday, November 26, 1885, Thanksgiving Day, Joseph Mathey held the grand opening of his new saloon, which he'd leased only the day before from one Peter O'Mara. Mathey's saloon was located in a two-story house on Center Street in Youngstown's neighboring industrial community of Hazelton. The room in the front on the first floor housed the bar and a pool table. The kitchen was located in a back room. Three rooms upstairs were used as sleeping apartments. Little did Mathey know that his saloon would be closed in only a few days and that a stain would blemish its reputation forever.

As a promotion to celebrate the holiday and to mark the grand opening, Mathey offered a raffle for turkeys and ducks. That evening, the saloon was full of drunken men, mostly mill workers and miners, many of whom were engaged in playing pool. As a man named Julius Gillman, a Belgian-born coal miner was taking his shot, he scratched, sending the little white cue ball flying off the table. At that very moment, a man named James Hey entered the saloon and made some rude comment to Gillman, Gillman returned a comment to Hey, and the altercation turned physical, with Hey striking Gillman. At this, a brawl ensued, during which, Gillman was struck over the back of the head with an oak cue stick, which broke into three pieces. Police were immediately summoned, and all of those who were in the saloon were taken into custody until the matter could be sorted. Julius Gillman was brought to one of the sleeping apartments upstairs, where he died from his injuries three hours later.

When questioned by police, Joseph Mathey attested that Gillman's assailant was James Rundle, a resident of Hubbard who worked at the nearby mill. The morning after the incident, James Rundle was charged with Gillman's murder. Rundle, meanwhile, maintained his innocence and said that it was James Hey who had struck the fatal blow with the cue stick. He would later go on to accuse another man, James Stone, of committing the heinous crime.

On December 22, Mathey's saloon now completely deserted, stories of a haunting began to emerge. Local residents of Hazelton, people of good repute, claimed that they heard strange noises about the place at night. Mill workers employed at the nearby Andrews Brothers and Co. Mill stated that, when walking home past the old saloon at night at the end of their shifts,

A view of Center Street in Hazelton reveals that most of the buildings no longer exist. *Photo by William G. Krejci.*

they would hear billiard balls rolling across the saloon's pool table and floor. Peter O'Mara, who owned the building and lived in a house across the street, shared that a week earlier, he was awakened by noises in the saloon that sounded much like people rolling heavy balls across the floor. He looked over toward the saloon, but all was dark, and he was so frightened that did not care to investigate the cause of the disturbance.

John Murphy, a young man who lived in the area, claimed that he'd walked past the saloon a few nights earlier and heard noises that sounded like chairs and tables being hurriedly moved about the floor. He looked inside, saw nothing and quickly fled the scene. Since the killing of Julius Gillman, the saloon had been dubbed The Slaughterhouse. This was the first time that the saloon had been empty in a long time. It was always known for having a rough reputation.

The following March, James Rundle was put on trial, charged with murder in the second degree. After a few days of testimony and blame being shifted by the accused to other people, the jury found Rundle guilty of assault and battery, not second-degree murder, as he'd been charged. This carried a maximum sentence of six months in the workhouse and a $200 fine, which Rundle received.

No address was ever given for the Hazelton saloon in which Julius Gillman was killed, thus it's very difficult to know where, exactly, the saloon was located. Perhaps, one day, that location will be discovered. Now a neighborhood of Youngstown, not much remains of Hazelton—certainly not the saloon.

9
The Ash Wednesday Ghost

41.771425, -81.627190

The only ghost I ever saw
Was dressed in mechlin,—so;
He wore no sandal on his foot,
And stepped like flakes of snow.
His gait was soundless, like the bird,
But rapid, like the roe;
His fashions quaint, mosaic,
Or, haply, mistletoe.
—*"The Only Ghost I Ever Saw," by Emily Dickinson*

In early March 1887, stories emerged that a farmhouse in the vicinity of the Stands Schoolhouse, being about five miles southwest of Massillon, was being haunted by the ghost of a man who had once owned the house and died there some years before.

The house in question had once belonged to John Altland and his family. Altland was born in York County, Pennsylvania, in May 1790. In 1817, he was married to Susanna Heckenroth, and shortly after, they moved to Stark County, Ohio, where they started a family. In 1846, the Altlands built their two-and-a-half-story brick house on what is presently Barr Street in Tuscarawas Township. It was in that house that John Altland died on July 17, 1871. He was laid to rest with his family at nearby Stanwood Cemetery.

According to the occupant of that house, an elderly German man known simply as Zog, the ghost of John Altland started appearing to him at all

A present-day view of the former John Altland House on Barrs Street. *Photo by Christina Johnson.*

hours of the day and night. Regarded as a relatively private man, Zog kept the visitations a secret for a very long time. Finally, when he could stand it no longer, he shared his secret with a man who worked for him. Even at that, he would share only that he was being haunted.

In time, the story of Zog being haunted in some manner came to the ears of a spiritualist, who took an interest in the case. Even though the spiritualist hired a translator, it was some time before the man came into Zog's confidence. When the spiritualist finally succeeded, Zog shared that the ghost of old man Altland insisted on staying with him, walking by his side, entering his chamber and almost residing with him. If Zog put out his hand to the spectral visitor, it would pass right through him. Yet the two never spoke to each other. At this, the spiritualist suggested that Zog attempt communication when the spirit next appeared, and Zog said that he'd do so.

Some time elapsed, and then, one night, Zog heard rapping sounds at his front door. He tried to ignore these but remembered that he said he'd attempt to talk to the ghost to see what he wanted. He gathered his courage and, upon answering the door, stepped out onto the front porch. There, the ghost of the elderly man appeared before him. He didn't say much, only that he would appear on the evening of Ash Wednesday, which was only a few days away.

Zog told his neighbors what he had witnessed and what the ghost had said regarding his next planned visit. When word reached Altland's son, likely Aaron Altland, who lived in nearby Massillon, he turned deeply pale and said that he had been haunted in the same way.

The evening of Ash Wednesday came, and with it came a throng of people to the old brick farmhouse. Zog explained to them that there had been some misunderstanding. The ghost had said he'd return on the eve of Ash Wednesday, being the previous night, and not Ash Wednesday's evening. Still, he related what the ghost had shared with him. The spirit said he had not died in his bed as many had believed; instead, he had been murdered on the front porch. He also said that he would return before long and would reveal many mysteries. But there was never a follow-up to the reports of John Altland's ghost appearing to Zog, so it's unknown if the ghost ever returned or revealed any mysteries.

10
The Clubhouse Ghost

41.500162, -81.688895

All houses wherein men have lived and died
are haunted houses. Through the open doors
The harmless phantoms on their errands glide,
With feet that make no sound upon the floors.
—"Haunted Houses," by Henry Wadsworth Longfellow

On January 23, 1888, a new ghostly sensation was reaching the ears of Clevelanders. It was reported that the new headquarters and clubhouse of the Cleveland Press Club, located in a former mansion at 127 Euclid Avenue, was in fact a haunted house. More than a dozen men were willing to testify that they had heard strange sounds and witnessed extraordinary sights about the club's parlors.

At three o'clock one morning, five reporters representing some of Cleveland's most prominent newspapers were playing pool in the billiard room when they heard a sharp knock at the door. One of the men was expecting a guest and sprang up to answer it, but when he opened the door, no one was in sight. Furthermore, it was snowing outside, yet no footprints were visible in the snow approaching the front door. Later, one of the billiard players felt a hard slap on his shoulder, but none of the other men in the room where anywhere near him. As their game drew to a close, the doorknob to the billiard room rattled vigorously. The men now suspected that someone was playing a joke on them. They rushed to the door and threw it open, but to quote Mr. Poe: "Darkness there and nothing more."

The Cleveland Press Club kept a clubhouse at 127 Euclid Avenue. *Photo courtesy the Western Reserve Historical Society.*

The next time the clubhouse was occupied late at night, the newspapermen invited three or four additional friends to join them. One of these guests leaned against the door that led from the billiard room to the hall. He claimed that there came three heavy knocks against the middle panel of the door. It was immediately thrown open, but the hall beyond was dark and empty. Later in the evening, a chandelier was seen shaking, and another inner door rattled violently, terrifying at least one guest.

The rooms of the clubhouse were seldom used during the day, and it was not stated whether any paranormal activity was witnessed before sundown. During the week leading up to the release of the story regarding the haunting of the Cleveland Press Club, there were said to be several disturbances. A young man representing a rural-area newspaper was shown through the rooms. He alleged that he heard groans and whistling coming from the back hallway. Another visitor stated that he saw a white-robed figure ascending the front steps late at night.

Henry Chisholm. *Library of Congress.*

Now, to understand a haunted house, it's best to look at the history of the place, and the history of this building is colorful to say the least. The beautiful Euclid Avenue home was built in 1857 for Nelson Monroe, a successful grocer and liquor merchant. The architects he chose to design his magnificent brick mansion were Charles Heard and Simeon Porter, the same firm that had recently rebuilt the famous Old Stone Church on Public Square, which had been devastated by a fire earlier that year. For many years, the Monroe house, which originally carried the address of 43 Euclid Street, was acknowledged as something of a local landmark. The walkway to the front door was flanked by two stone greyhounds that seemed to catch everyone's attention.

Nelson Monroe was born in January 1810 in Bridgewater, Oneida County, New York. At about the age of twenty, he came to Cleveland, where, in time, he married Mary E. Luther. In all, they had six children, but only their eldest, Mary Keokee Monroe, who went by her middle name, lived beyond infancy.

On June 24, 1860, Nelson Monroe died quite suddenly from tuberculosis at the age of fifty. His funeral was held from his beautiful residence, and he was laid to rest at nearby Erie Street Cemetery. Upon his death, the house was deeded to his daughter, Keokee, then only eleven years of age. Three years later, through her guardian, Martin B. Scott, Keokee sold the house to Cleveland industrialist Henry Chisholm for $29,025.

Sadly, Mary Keokee Monroe took ill in very early 1866, and her health began to rapidly fail. She died on January 23, 1866, at the age of seventeen.

In 1869, the deceased members of the Monroe family, those being Nelson, Keokee and her siblings who'd died in infancy, were exhumed from Erie Street Cemetery and reinterred in a new family plot at Woodland Cemetery. A large marble statue of an angel, which bears a striking resemblance to Mary Keokee Monroe, was placed at the grave site. The angel holds a shield that depicts a profile of the girl's likeness. The edge of the shield carries her final dying words: "When I go over the river, I shall sing." The shield rests

Left: Mary Keokee Monroe. *From* The Uncertainty of Life, *by Reverend A.H. Strong, 1866.*

Opposite: Mary Keokee Monroe's monument at Cleveland's Woodland Cemetery is adorned with flowers in tribute. *Photo by William G. Krejci.*

on a pedestal, upon which the name "Keokee" is engraved. The statue's base carries the phrase: "She blooms in the fields of light."

To further honor her daughter's memory, Mrs. Monroe, who was a frequent vacationer to the Poconos, donated $9,000 to a congregation in Paradise Valley, Pennsylvania, for the construction of a chapel and grounds for a cemetery. Completed in 1894, Keokee Chapel United Methodist Church still stands on Keokee Chapel Lane.

Regarding Chisholm…

Born in Lochgelly, Fife, Scotland, in 1822, Henry Chisholm came to Cleveland in 1850 by way of Montreal. He first worked at building docks and piers around the city, most of which were constructed for the railroads. Within a few years, Chisholm had amassed enough money to invest in a steel firm, which, when reorganized in 1862, became the Cleveland Rolling Mill Company. Chisholm served as its vice president and general superintendent. At about the age of seventeen, he married Jean Allen of Dunfirmline, Scotland, and the two raised eight children together.

Henry Chisholm died at his home on Euclid on May 9, 1881, following a three-week illness. His funeral was held from his residence, which now carried the address 408 Euclid Avenue. It was said that more than four

thousand employees from his rolling mill filed passed his home during the funeral. Chisholm was originally interred at Woodland Cemetery but was ultimately laid to rest in a new family mausoleum at Lakeview, the largest in the cemetery. A larger-than-life statue of the Cleveland industrialist can also be found at Lakeview Cemetery.

Though built by Nelson Monroe in 1857, the house that would one day gain a reputation for being haunted while under the ownership of the Cleveland Press Club would always be known as the old Chisholm mansion.

In 1887, the house passed from Chisholm's widow to the Cleveland Press Club, which would endure some rather hair-raising experiences in its time at that address (two years earlier, it had been changed to 127 Euclid Avenue). The club's time in the house, however, was brief. The Cleveland Press Club folded in 1889. For a time after, the house was used as the dining parlors for the Philadelphia Dairy and Café Company, but within a couple of years, it saw use again as a private residence. In 1895, the house was demolished and replaced by a high-rise commercial structure called the New England Building, later known as the National City Bank Building. At more than 220 feet tall, it was the tallest building in Cleveland until 1922. Today, it carries the address 623 Euclid Avenue. The site of the haunted clubhouse, formerly occupied by the Monroe and Chisholm families, is today occupied by an upscale restaurant called The Marble Room.

11

The Ghostly Woman on Bolivar Street

41.499113, -81.681925

Oh, very gloomy is the house of woe,
Where tears are falling while the bell is knelling,
With all the dark solemnities that show,
That Death is in the dwelling!
—The Haunted House, *by Thomas Hood*

One of Cleveland's most striking—and rumored to also be one of its most haunted—buildings is by far Grays Armory on Bolivar Road downtown. Many find themselves, in passing, staring up at its imposing turret and narrow windows, wondering what it's history and lore might be.

This remarkable building is home to the Cleveland Grays, a local military organization with roots that go back to the days when Cleveland was little more than a few decades old. The Cleveland Grays was established in 1837 as the Cleveland City Guard, an independent military organization. The following year, it took the name The Cleveland Grays for the color of the uniforms its members wore, which, it is said, emulated those worn by the cadets at West Point Military Academy in New York. It should be noted that the current armory wasn't its first.

When still known as the Cleveland City Guard in 1837, the organization kept a small armory located in the Commercial Buildings block at 59–63 Superior Street. Within a few months, it relocated its armory to the Farmers' Block on the northeast corner of Ontario and Prospect Streets. The building was also known as Gray's Military Hall. By the time of the Civil War, the organization had relocated to Lyman's Block at 158 Superior Street, just west of Monument Square, now known as Public Square. Between 1871 and 1880, it kept its armory at 25 Frankfort Street. Today the site is marked by the building at 620 Frankfort Avenue. From around 1881 to 1892, Grays Armory was located on Long Street. That armory burned in 1892, which facilitated the need for a new building. The location of that last armory is now the site of the former U.S. Post Office building at 1500 West 3rd Street. The current Grays Armory, built in the Romanesque Revival style, was erected in 1893 at 48 Bolivar Street, today's address being 1234 Bolivar Road, between Erie Street (later renamed East 9th Street) and Prospect Avenue.

The Grays witnessed and added to a large part of American history. It was the first military company from Cleveland to volunteer to fight in the Civil War. During that conflict, the company saw action at the Battle of First Manassas and the defense of Washington, D.C., against General Jubal A. Early's troops in 1864. It also participated in military operations during the Spanish-American War and World War I. Many members individually served in military actions from World War II through the Gulf War. Today, the Grays' mission is to promote patriotism and military history in Cleveland and to preserve the armory that has served as the company's home for more than 130 years.

The armory, too, saw quite a bit of action in its remarkable existence. It witnessed the first concert given by the newly organized Cleveland Orchestra in 1918. It was also chosen as the location to host the first auto show held in Cleveland.

A remarkable history, true. But what of the ghost stories?

Those are masterfully covered in the book *Haunted Cleveland*, by Beth A. Richards and Chuck L. Gove, a must-own for anyone who has an interest in Cleveland ghost stories. To briefly recap, the armory, it is said, is haunted by numerous spirits. One that is considered quite mischievous is the ghost that is referred to as Patrick. It's said Patrick loves to play pranks on various members of the Grays, as well as visitors and contractors. Another is believed to be the ghost of Major Lou Grosser, who was in charge of Grays Armory for a number of years. It is said that the smell of vanilla pipe tobacco, his favorite blend, can be experienced in the drill hall. Others have witnessed a man in military uniform lingering in various places throughout the armory.

One story that is not covered is the report of a ghostly woman in white. One might ask: Why would the ghost of a woman haunt a building that

Grays Armory on Bolivar Road in Cleveland. Notice the houses located to the right. *Library of Congress.*

has historically been the home of a men's military organization? Again, it's advisable to look into the history of the site rather than the building itself. That history tells us that, prior to the construction of the armory in 1893, the site was occupied by a row of houses. What stories do they tell? Tragic ones, unfortunately.

In all, seven houses were ultimately demolished to make way for Grays Armory, four for the building itself and another three where the parking lot to the west now sits. There were numerous deaths throughout these houses' existence, but two stand out more than the others.

On the evening of Friday, December 17, 1869, George H. McKay and his family were hosting a gathering at their residence at 136 Bolivar Street. Music, conversation and refreshments were the highlights of the evening. In the dining room sat the servant girl, Irish-born Kate Touhey, aged twenty-

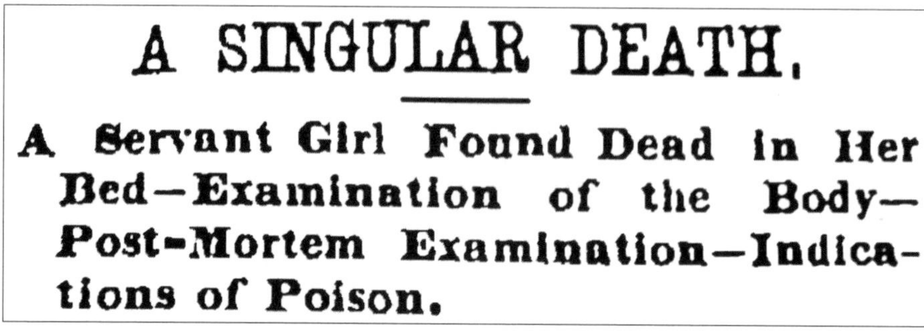

A SINGULAR DEATH.

A Servant Girl Found Dead in Her Bed—Examination of the Body—Post-Mortem Examination—Indications of Poison.

A headline announces the death of Kate Touhey's poisoning. *From the* Cleveland Leader, *December 20, 1869.*

five years. Orphaned at an early age, she'd come to this country three years earlier with her sister, Mary.

Shortly after eleven o'clock, the guests departed, and the McKay family retired to bed while Kate cleaned up. Customarily, the servant would wake up early, get the fires going, prepare breakfast and then call the family down once it was all ready. Curiously, Kate Touhey made no appearance that morning. The fireplaces were cold, and no breakfast was placed on the table. Having heard no call for breakfast, a member of the family went to the servant's room and discovered her cold and lifeless body lying in bed. The family was shocked and horrified at the sudden death of the girl. Aside from a slight amount of vomit on her bed, she appeared as she had the previous evening, with no sign of sickness otherwise.

The coroner was notified, and Drs. Cleveland and Brooks were sent for. Upon the arrival of coroner J.C. Schenck, a postmortem examination of the corpse was made. It was found that the woman's stomach was in a highly inflamed state and that some corrosive poison had been taken. It was the opinion of the doctors that oxalic acid had been ingested. The family insisted that no such substance was kept in the house—nor was any other poison for that matter. A search of the house was made, and no chemical matching that which had been taken could be found.

There appeared to be no reason for Kate Touhey to take her own life. Her sister, Mary, who was also questioned, stated that she never knew of her sister having a moment's trouble, and she believed that Kate had never been melancholy at any point during her life. Her disposition was very lively and gay. From morning to night, her voice was heard ringing through the house, and her laughing face provoked good humor in everyone she met.

No one could understand how she came to be poisoned. She had eaten much of the same food the family had. The night of the party, she'd eaten

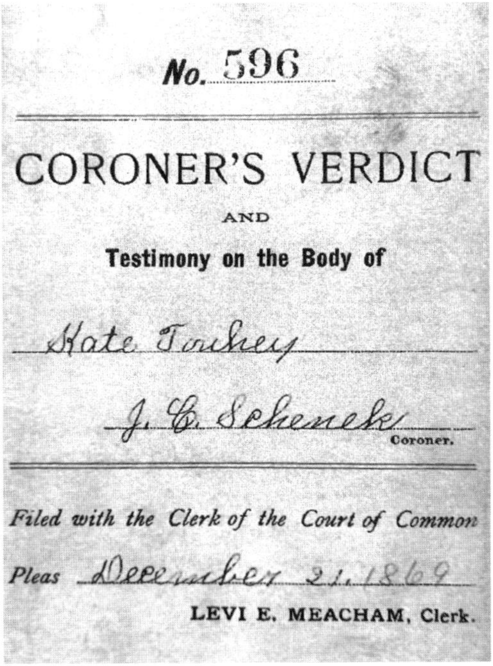

No. 596

CORONER'S VERDICT

AND

Testimony on the Body of

Kate Touhey

J. C. Schenck

Coroner.

Filed with the Clerk of the Court of Common Pleas December 21, 1869

LEVI E. MEACHAM, Clerk.

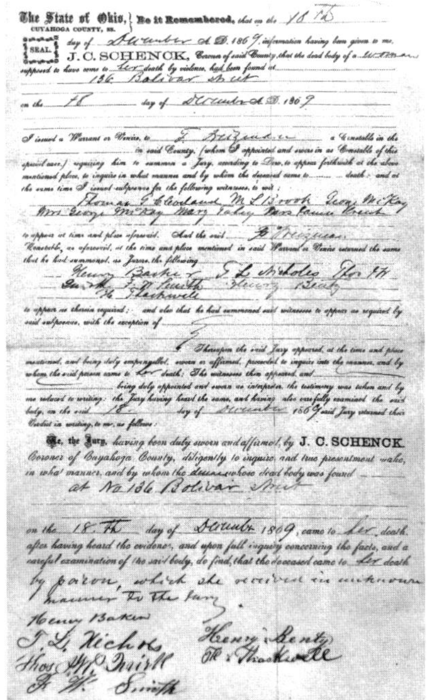

The State of Ohio, CUYAHOGA COUNTY, ss. Be it Remembered, that on the 18th day of December A.D. 1869, information having been given to me, J. C. SCHENCK, Coroner of said County, that the dead body of a woman supposed to have come to her death by violence, had been found at 136 Bolivar Street on the 18 day of December A.D. 1869

SEAL.

I issued a Warrant or Venire, to [illegible] a Constable in the in said County, (whom I appointed and swore in as Constable of this special case,) requiring him to summon a Jury, according to Law, to appear forthwith at the above mentioned place, to inquire in what manner and by whom the deceased came to ...... death: and at the same time I issued subpoenas for the following witnesses, to wit: Thomas [illegible] Cleveland, M. L. Brooks, Geo. McKay, Mrs. George McKay, Mary Fahey, [illegible]

to appear at time and place aforesaid. And the said [illegible] Constable, as aforesaid, at the time and place mentioned in said Warrant or Venire returned the same that he had summoned, as Jurors, the following Henry Barker, T. L. Nicholes, Thos. [illegible], F. W. Smith, Henry Beaty, H. Thackwell

to appear as therein required; and also that he had summoned said witnesses to appear as required by said subpoenas, with the exception of

Thereupon the said Jury appeared, at the time and place mentioned, and being duly empanelled, sworn or affirmed, proceeded to inquire into the manner, and by whom the said person came to her death: The witnesses then appeared, and being duly appointed and sworn as interpreter, the testimony was taken and by me reduced to writing: the Jury having heard the same, and having also carefully examined the said body, on the said 18 day of December 1869 said Jury returned their Verdict in writing, to me, as follows:

We, the Jury, having been duly sworn and affirmed, by J. C. SCHENCK, Coroner of Cuyahoga County, diligently to inquire and true presentment make, in what manner, and by whom the deceased whose dead body was found at No 136 Bolivar Street

on the 18th day of December 1869, came to her death after having heard the evidence, and upon full inquiry concerning the facts, and a careful examination of the said body, do find, that the deceased came to her death by poison, which she received in unknown manner to the Jury.

Henry Baker
T. L. Nichols
Thos. [illegible]
F. W. Smith
Henry Beaty
H. Thackwell

Left: The cover page for the Cuyahoga County coroner's report for case no. 596. *Courtesy of the Cuyahoga County Archives.*

Right: The Cuyahoga County coroner's report for case no. 596, which states that Kate Touhey died from poison she received in an "unknown manner." *Courtesy of the Cuyahoga County Archives.*

only some cake and apples, nothing more. Some had suspected that she'd recently visited a pharmacist to obtain salts for medicinal purposes but had accidentally been given the acid. Few suspected foul play.

In the end, the verdict of the coroner's jury was simply "that the deceased came to her death by poison, which she received in unknown manner to the jury." Kate Touhey's funeral was held on Sunday, December 19, 1869, at St. John's Cathedral.

Curiously, a very similar death was reported on the future site of Grays Armory twenty-five years later.

On Friday, April 25, 1884, Ann McClosky, an estimable woman of thirty-five years, died at the home of her parents at 144 Bolivar Street. For ten years, she had suffered from a nervous condition, and on Friday evening, she was found to be in a state of severe discomfort. It was soon discovered that she had ingested a significant amount of aqua ammonia. Drs. J.H. Lowman and J.W. Sapp were sent for, but upon their arrival, it was realized that the patient was beyond relief. The liquid had completely cauterized her lips, throat and stomach. She died while asleep after a few hours of terrible suffering.

Miss McClosky was given to frequent headaches, and it was supposed that she'd taken the ammonia by mistake instead of the medicine that had been prescribed to her by her physician, Dr. Sapp. The doctor refused to tell reporters what had caused her death, and the manner in which he spoke on the subject tended to surround it with mystery. Miss McClosky's family were also disinclined to speak on her death. Dr. Sapp ultimately reported to the health office on the matter, stating that Ann McClosky's death was caused by "nervous prostration and weakness," not by poisoning from aqua ammonia. No autopsy was performed, and no coroner's case file exists. Ann McClosky was laid to rest at St. Joseph Cemetery on Woodland Avenue.

Now, most Cleveland ghost enthusiasts are well aware of the haunting of Grays Armory. And while this may say something of tragic deaths regarding women on the site of the armory, it still begs the question: where does the forgotten haunting aspect of this story come into play?

On June 10, 1889, just five years after the tragic death of Ann McClosky, the *Plain Dealer* reported that there was a haunted house located on Bolivar Street, between Erie and Prospect Streets.

The specter, according to the paper, had taken lodgings there a couple of months earlier, and she was satisfied in roaming the house at midnight, using her voice a great deal. The reporter who covered the story was very clear in expressing the fact that the ghostly visitor was a woman. Occupants of the house reported late night rappings on the walls and a low, moaning voice crying, "Oh, dear! Oh, dear!" in a way that made their blood chill.

A lady in the house felt a chilly grasp on her shoulder one night that sent an indescribable thrill of horror through her. The ghost was also heard to wail out, screaming, "You have gone too far to retract!" A gentleman who was going into the house one night saw an apparition of a woman at the foot of the staircase. It stood still for a moment while he gazed at it, and then it disappeared with a rustling sound, melting out of sight. He then felt a faint, chilly motion in the air.

As no names or an address are given in the report, it's impossible to know where, exactly, this house was located. Still, only a small handful of houses were standing at the time in the location described. It's speculative, but there's a good chance that it was one of the seven houses that were torn down in 1893 to make way for the armory. Prior to this revelation, many believed that the ghostly woman in white at Grays Armory had wandered in from neighboring Erie Street Cemetery immediately to the south. Weighing the evidence, it's now believed that there may be another reason for her presence.

On a personal note—and I rarely insert myself into a story—I would like to take a moment to share an experience of my own. As it turns out, your author spent some time at this location as a youth.

For a number of years, my parents were members of the Western Reserve Theatre Organ Society, the 501(c)(3) nonprofit local chapter of the American Theatre Organ Society. This organization has its offices at Grays Armory, where it also cares for the 1931 Wurlitzer theater organ that is owned by the Grays. That beautiful instrument was moved to the armory in 1970 from the Warner Theatre in Erie, Pennsylvania.

I recall that, around 1990, I was off from school for about a week. During that time, my parents were at the armory, tuning the organ before an upcoming concert. I had accompanied them down there and found myself sitting in the office by myself on the second floor at the back of the building. I was fond of drawing at the time and carried a sketchpad and pencils with me most everywhere I went.

At the time, I was deeply engrossed in sketching out the view of Erie Street Cemetery and a small family mausoleum that stood just on the other side of the sandstone wall. I suddenly heard the door to the office open and slam closed. Thinking that it was my mother, I turned around but found the room empty. I soon realized that I could hear both of my parents still tuning the organ, my father in the chamber with the pipes and my mother on the keyboard, playing each pipe that was being tuned. I stepped into the hallway but found that the rest of the place was empty.

Unfortunately, that's the extent of my ghostly encounters at Grays Armory. I never experienced any of the previously mentioned paranormal events that others had; I didn't even see the woman in white, whoever she may be.

12
The Ghost with the Brogue

41.483273, -81.702867

Poetry, music, I have loved, and yet
Because of those new dead
That come into my soul and escape
Confusion of the bed,
Or those begotten or unbegotten
Perning in a band,
I bend my body to the spade
Or grope with a dirty hand.
—*"The Spirit Medium," by William Butler Yeats*

Cleveland has seen its share of colorful characters come and go, but few hold a candle to Dr. Andrew W.S. Rothermel, the noted medium.

Born in Germany on March 24, 1848, Andrew Rothermel immigrated with his parents and six siblings to the United States in the late 1850s and settled in Brooklyn, New York, where he ended up working for a number of years as a barber. In 1868, he was wed to Miss Adelia Elias, but in 1877, the two divorced. Shortly after, he married Priscilla C. Smith, with whom he had five children.

Around 1880, Rothermel started practicing spiritual mediumship. Five years later, he started introducing himself as "Doctor" Rothermel. He would later falsely claim to be a medical doctor. After extensive travels across the Northeast and Midwest, presenting his abilities in the otherworldly arts, he made his way to Cleveland, where he arrived in the late spring of 1889.

The building at 2066–2074 West 25th Street, where Dr. Rothermel contacted spirits from beyond the grave, circa 1944. *Photo courtesy of the Cleveland Public Library Photograph Collection.*

On the evening of June 27, a number of people gathered in the rooms occupied by one Mrs. Marquette at 639 Pearl Street on Cleveland's West Side. This would be, if you will, Dr. Andrew W.S. Rothermel's closing act of a brief performance on Ohio's north coast.

The evening began with Dr. Rothermel repeating a number of tests that had previously been administered, proving his psychic abilities. He then had the room darkened, and to everyone's great satisfaction, he was able to materialize a number of spirits from the other side. Most of these spirits stepped out from a cabinet in the room, robed in the traditional white, and strolled around those seated about the room, who greatly marveled at the experience. At other points throughout the night, Dr. Rothermel was personally controlled by a few spirits, though none were nearly as memorable as the ghost who spoke with a thick Irish brogue. The crowd who had gathered entertained this spirit, appeasing him by singing songs like "Nearer My God to Thee" and "In the Sweet By and By." Feeling quite satisfied that they had touched the world beyond the veil, the attendees departed Mrs. Marquette's rooms around midnight. It was one of Dr. Rothermel's most successful séances.

An illustration making a poor joke out of a séance where an Irish ghost is raised. *Library of Congress.*

To truly understand Dr. Rothermel's time in Cleveland, we have to go back to the beginning of June 1889, when he first arrived and took up rooms in the home of Dr. Ferris at 207 Prospect Street, now 833 Prospect Avenue. On June 4, about twenty-five ladies and gentlemen joined the doctor to witness a spiritual séance. Once Dr. Rothermel was securely tied up and seated in a chair, the entertainment began. Hands were manifest from behind a curtain, a music box opened and played on its own accord and items seemed to magically materialize from behind the same curtain that produced the manifesting hands. Near the end of the evening, a number of questions were asked of Dr. Rothermel regarding the spirit world. At one point, someone asked him about little Maggie Thompson.

The daughter of Jacob and Clara Thompson of 24 Merchant Street, seven-year-old Maggie had gone missing back on May 9 while on her way home from school to have lunch. She never arrived. A frantic search of the area was made, but no sign of the girl could be found. It had been nearly a month now, and hope of finding her alive was dwindling fast.

Dr. Rothermel replied to the query regarding the Thompson girl, claiming that he could find her by using "psychometry" if he had an article of hers.

He explained that it worked by divining a direction, much like a compass. Instead of using magnetism, however, a needle would register the psychic influence that the girl had left on an article of clothing or the like. Once the needle pointed in a certain direction, he would set off to another location and take a second reading. He'd then take a third reading at another location and tally all the results together to triangulate her position.

A few days later, Mrs. Thompson went to Dr. Rothermel's rooms at 207 Prospect Street and invited him to her home to try out his psychometry experiment. Once there, she handed him one of Maggie's dolls, which none of the other children had handled. From the observations of his test, all indications pointed to the girl being located somewhere northeast of the Thompson home. Upon his departure, Dr. Rothermel was met by a reporter, with whom he shared the results of the test, saying that he would make further observations the next day, somewhere in the east and southeast, until he could pinpoint her location. He concluded by stating that he'd found many bodies in that manner. It was sad to think that he was already concluding the little girl was dead.

It's not known if Rothermel made those further observations the next day. What is known is that, that evening, he held another séance in his rooms on Prospect Street. Here, he introduced Clevelanders to spirit telegraphy. Rothermel claimed that he could receive messages from the other side via a special machine that was controlled by a spirit operator. The machine didn't work as well as most had hoped, so Rothermel brought forth the spirit of a woman named Emma that sang—you guessed it—"In the Sweet By and By."

Two nights later, the badly decomposed body of Maggie Thompson was discovered in the basement of the house at 42 Merchant Avenue, now West 11th Street. The house was occupied by the Lueth family. Within a short time, police arrested Mr. and Mrs. Lueth's sixteen-year-old son, Otto, and charged him with murder, to which he soon confessed. Otto Lueth was convicted of murder and executed by hanging the following summer.

It should be noted that the house where Maggie Thompson's remains were discovered was nine houses to the south of the Thompson's home on Merchant Street, not northeast, as Dr. Rothermel had claimed his tests indicated.

Shortly after that final late June séance at Mrs. Marquette's rooms on Pearl Street, Dr. Rothermel departed Cleveland and returned to New York. Within a couple of years, he moved west. In time, Dr. Rothermel became something of a legend at divining the locations of valuable minerals and

A present-day view of 2066–2074 West 25th Street. *Photo by William G. Krejci.*

the like. Before long, he was referring to himself as a mine expert and spiritual scientist. In 1896, he was looking for gold in Nebraska. The following year, he was locating valuable ore in Minnesota. By 1911, he was working out in California, where he was divining the location of oil in San Bernardino. Later that year, he was working in the Arizona desert, searching for water.

Dr. Andrew W.S. Rothermel died on August 10, 1922, in Milwaukee, Wisconsin. He was buried at Forest Home Cemetery, where his headstone informs us that he has "passed on to the higher life." The building that housed Mrs. Marquette's rooms, which once saw the visitation of a ghost with a brogue speaking through the illustrious Dr. Rothermel, still stands at 2068 West 25th Street.

13

The Last House on Maud Avenue

40.773445, -82.519000

There was a moment during which I listened, reminded of the faint sense I had had, the first night, of there being something undefinably astir in the house, and noted the soft breath of the open casement just move the half-drawn blind.
—The Turn of the Screw, *by Henry James*

It's always that creepy old house at the end of the street that seems to be the haunted one—the one that, as children, we tend to avoid. This appeared to be the case on little Maud Avenue in Mansfield back in March 1892.

Jeremiah "Jerry" Bird was born in February 1859 in Mt. Gilead, Ohio. At the age of six, he moved with his parents and extensive family to Mansfield and seemed to have a typical upbringing. Newspaper articles claim that, in 1879, he married nineteen-year-old Anna Gandert of Mansfield while in a state of intoxication. His parents objected to the marriage and appeared to make things difficult for him. The two lived together on and off for some time, even staying with Anna's family on occasion. Still, there appeared to be a rift between them that grew wider as the years progressed. In 1887, Jerry Bird was granted a divorce on the grounds of adultery.

Soon after, he took a job working as a night clerk at a hotel in Tiffin, but a few months later, found himself in Zanesville, where he married Maxine B. Harris. Soon after, they returned to Mansfield and took up residency on Maud Avenue. The house they selected was on the east side of the street, where it ended a block north of Harker Street. It was otherwise designated as sub-lot 1597 of Dailey and Reed's subdivision.

A historic view of 556 North Mulberry Street, formerly Maud Avenue, in Mansfield. *Photo courtesy of the Richland County Auditor's Office.*

Jerry Bird mended ties with his family, and everyone seemed to like Maxine, particularly Jerry's father, a man of advanced age named William Eli Bird. Sadly, Jerry's father passed away on May 7, 1891. Not long after, things around Jerry and Maxine's house started to get a little weird.

Apparently, the Birds were unaware that the house they had moved into carried a reputation of being haunted. Once they were made aware of it, they likely brushed it off. But then one night, not even a year after the death of Jerry's father, Maxine Bird awoke to an unusual but familiar noise. It was the sound of a rocking chair moving back and forth.

Following the death of William Bird, Jerry's mother gifted the Birds her late husband's rocking chair, which had been one of her husband's favorite pieces of furniture. It was now after midnight, and Maxine could distinctly hear that chair moving. Surely someone was sitting in it. She got out of bed and made her way over to the chair, where, to her great astonishment, she came face to face with the specter of her late father-in-law.

Ever since that encounter, strange and peculiar noises were heard about the house in the dead of night. A reporter for the *Mansfield Weekly News* dismissed these as the result of having an exposed house that stood without shelter and blamed the appearance of the ghost and the curious noises on the March winds.

At the time, Jerry and Maxine Bird had only one child, their daughter, Julia, or Lulu, as they called her, who was just a little over two years old. Four more children would be added to the family in the years to come but not in that house. Shortly after the disturbances were reported, the family moved to 144 Woodland Avenue, and then a few years later, they moved to Ritter Street, which is now Sturges Avenue. In 1900, they moved out of Mansfield altogether and took up residency in Shelby, Ohio.

Jerry Bird died in 1921 in Sandusky, where he was buried at Oakland Cemetery. Maxine joined him twelve years later.

As for the last house on Maud Avenue, it didn't remain that way for very long. In time, Maud Avenue was extended a few blocks to the north, where it now terminates at West Longview Avenue. Upon making the extension, the name of the street was changed from Maud Avenue to North Mulberry Street, and the house was given the address 556 North Mulberry Street. In recent years, the house sat empty and became a derelict structure. It very much looked like a haunted house of legend. Sadly, it was demolished around 2017. All that remains today is an empty lot on the southeast corner of North Mulberry Street and Chester Avenue.

A present-day view of the empty lot at 556 North Mulberry Street in Mansfield, where the haunted house on Maud Avenue once stood. *Photo by William G. Krejci.*

14

THE HOUSE ON EMERALD ALLEY

41.504951, -81.686697

It was a haunted house! There it stood, in all its faded gentility, in all its gloominess and loneliness, and it was incontestably haunted! The neighbors said so; almost everybody said so, and what almost everybody said, especially about the greatest mystery in Bleak Alley, was not without its weight.
—Shot Through the Heart, *by Henry S. Doane*

Emerald Alley, in Cleveland, looked much like any other side street in the downtown area. Running northeast to southwest between Dodge and Muirson Streets, it was a long and narrow lane, being only about 18 feet wide but almost 1,800 feet in length, and was paved in red brick. Surely, nobody would ever have given Emerald Alley a second thought—if not for the fact that it also contained a haunted house.

There were quite a few houses that faced out onto the little thoroughfare. Though these houses fronted the alley, their addresses corresponded with the homes that faced the main streets behind them; this designated them as rear homes. Our next story took place in late October 1892 at 67 Oregon Street, Rear.

The house in question was a two-story frame house, painted brown, and it contained about eight rooms. With the exception of a very brief tenant, the house had been empty since the death of its last occupant back in January 1892. The house behind it, the one that faced Oregon Street, was said to have been occupied by a respectable family who had nothing to hinder their contentment with the neighborhood—until the paranormal activity in the house behind them started.

An illustration of the haunted house on Emerald Court. *From the* Cleveland Press, *October 27, 1892.*

The most recent occupant of the haunted house was an aged gentleman who had briskly moved out just six weeks earlier. One evening, while he was preparing his supper, the man heard a noise coming from an upstairs bedroom that sounded very much like an intoxicated man sleeping off the effects of a heavy bender. The man rushed out to the street, where he flagged down a patrolman named Dolan and explained what was occurring. The patrolman followed him back into the house, listened for a moment and also heard the sounds coming from upstairs. He agreed that it sounded very much like a sleeping drunken man. Dolan was about to send for a patrol wagon when he heard a loud groan coming from the bedroom. He realized then that it may in fact be someone suffering from a physical injury, not too much liquor as they'd first thought.

The two men ran up the stairs to investigate, but with each step they took, the sounds grew quieter and quieter. When they reached the top of the stairs, the sounds stopped entirely. All the rooms were empty. A thorough search was made, but no sign of a man or any other human could be detected. Every window was sealed, and there appeared to be no way that anyone could have escaped. The following morning, that elderly gentleman moved out.

Since that time, strange sounds were heard issuing from the house, but out of fear of ridicule, few shared their experiences with anyone other than close friends, family and confidants. One such witness was a man named Thomas Connor, a meat dealer who kept his business on nearby Saint Clair Street. While making deliveries shortly before dawn, he and a friend rode passed the alleged haunted house, where they heard a long and drawn out scream of agony in a woman's voice, followed by the cry of "Murder!" They waited for no more than that; they cracked the whip and urged the horses away from the scene as fast as they could pull the cart. Police were immediately notified, but again, a complete search of the house turned up no sign of human activity. It was as vacant and undisturbed as it always presented itself in daylight.

A watchman named Daniel McClusky, who walked the beat in that neighborhood, first noticed peculiar sounds issuing from the house about two weeks earlier. Neighbors told him that they, too, had witnessed these sounds. Moans, groans, screams, sighs and rappings were the most commonly reported sounds.

As it turned out, the house first gained a reputation for being haunted a few years earlier, but not much publicity of the paranormal activity was made, and the stories soon dwindled. Now that the stories were being published in newspapers, the house started to draw large crowds who stood in front of it nightly to watch for ghostly activity. Those who had congregated paid particular attention the upper left bedroom window, which was said to be the ghost's room.

The haunted room where the ghostly activity was at its greatest. *From the* Cleveland Press, *October 27, 1892.*

An elderly resident of Oregon Street who had joined in with the crowd was quite surprised that no report of the haunting had been published until that point. Most of the neighbors, many of whom were regarded as very respectable people, knew the home's reputation and were witness to the strange sounds that were heard at night.

"Such is the feeling that these stories have inspired," explained the elderly resident, "that children and women will not pass the house after nightfall and when the hour has grown late, men, too, pass it with trepidation."

Another man, a plasterer named John Burk, came forward and shared his experience with the house.

> *I never told the story before because I was afraid of ridicule, but it is true. Sunday night, I had occasion to pass by the haunted house at a very late hour. I did not know then it was haunted and expected to see nothing unusual. In front of the building, I stopped to light my pipe and turned to the opposite fence to strike a match, when right behind me, proceeding from the upper windows of the house, I heard half-suffocated breathings and groans that nearly froze my blood. I turned and looked towards the house. The door, which was closed, slowly opened and then closed again softly, but nothing whatever came out. Then I ran, not stopping until I reached Erie Street.*

Evidently, there was a story being told about the house that gave an explanation for why it would have been haunted. It was claimed that the house was once occupied by a milkman named Ryan. Several years earlier, he died quite suddenly while apparently in the best of health. The cause of his death was a puzzle, and the doctor's diagnosis was not in accord with the opinions of the neighbors. Immediately after—and just as suddenly and with as little cause—his wife died.

Almost every haunted house, it seems, carries some back story that speaks of tragedy and loss. Why should the haunted house on Emerald Alley be any different? Thorough research reveals who the Ryans really were.

John J. Ryan was born in 1840 in Tipperary, Ireland. He came to the United States with his family and settled in Cleveland. In 1866, he purchased from James and Jane Greene the southern half of lot 43, which would eventually have the haunted house occupying the lot behind it. Two years later, he was married to Mary H. Purcell, also from Ireland. John Ryan worked for some time as a railroad engineer, but in the early 1880s, became a milk dealer. He died on August 5, 1887, from rheumatism of the heart. John Ryan was fifty-two years old.

The following year, the rear house was occupied by John's widowed mother, Ann Ryan. Also living with her was a woman named Jane Nunn. The front house continued to be occupied by John's widow, at least until her death at the age of forty-nine, which occurred on August 14, 1888, just over a year after her husband's passing. Mary Ryan's cause of death was phthisis pulmonalis, or pulmonary tuberculosis. They left behind five children, the youngest of whom was only eight. John and Mary Ryan were buried together at St. John Cemetery on Woodland Avenue.

It should be noted that, with the brief exception of John's widowed mother in 1888, the Ryan family lived in the house to the south that fronted Oregon Street, not the haunted house behind it that fronted Emerald Alley.

As for the actual haunted house that sat on the back half of that property, the house was occupied for about a decade by the Cranley family. John and Honora Cranley took up residency in that house in early 1870, having moved there from just up the street at 102 California Alley. Sadly, John, who also worked as a milkman, died at the home on February 22, 1871. He was followed to the grave by his eighteen-year-old daughter, Mary, three months later. Both died from consumption. Honora Cranley continued to occupy the house with her surviving children through early 1880.

Following the departure of the Cranley family, the house was rented to Anthony and Anna Born, who lived there very briefly with their three young children, but they abruptly moved out after a year. The house sat empty for the next few years, but from 1886 to 1888, it was rented on and off to various tenants, many of whom didn't stay very long.

The last occupant of the house, who had lived there before the brief stay of the aged gentleman in 1892, was Catherine Coyne, the widow of John, who had died back in September 1881. It was also occupied by her sons, Patrick and John, and a boarder named Charles Quelch. Catherine Coyne resided in the house for four years until her abrupt death from consumption on January 24, 1892, at the age of forty-seven. The haunting was reported only nine months later.

By all indications, the house at 67 Oregon Street, Rear, was torn down shortly after the reports of the haunting emerged.

In the end, Oregon Street was ultimately renamed Rockwell Avenue. Emerald Alley still exists as Emerald Court, but the section that contained the haunted house was eliminated entirely around 1979, when a high-rise building called St. Clair Place was built over the middle of it. No trace of the house, nor the section of Emerald Alley that it sat on, remains. Today, the specific site of the house is occupied by a parking lot on the east side of East 12th Street, between Rockwell and Saint Clair Avenues.

15

A DEN OF THIEVES

41.496346, -81.706362

And still of a winter's night, they say, when the wind is in the trees,
When the moon is a ghostly galleon tossed upon cloudy seas,
When the road is a ribbon of moonlight over the purple moor,
A highwayman comes riding—
Riding—riding—
A highwayman comes riding, up to the old inn-door.
—"The Highwayman," by Alfred Noyes

When most people go out to celebrate New Year's Eve, they usually do so in the company of friends and loved ones, but typically, they celebrate in a local pub or at a friend's house. Not many would select an abandoned haunted house as their gathering spot, but that's exactly what three men decided to do on December 31, 1892.

At a late hour of the evening, a Cleveland patrolman named Pillars witnessed a young man crawling out of the window of William McIntyre's Saloon at 143 Main Street, near the top of the West Bank of the Flats by present-day West 25th Street. The man appeared to have a suspicious-looking bundle under his arm. He followed the man down the street, to the bottom of the hill, where he approached the three-story brick house at 48 Main Street, and he watched as the man crawled in through a cellar door at the rear of the building.

Patrolman Pillars tried the side door but found it locked from within. He ultimately crawled into the cellar through the back but found it to be empty. Through a crack in the floor, he observed a light and heard voices conversing above. Making his way up two sets of stairs, he found himself on an upper level of the building that had been floored using old wooden doors laid across the rafters. There, he saw three men huddled around a new stove that had been placed up there. The suspicious package turned out to be a basket containing several stolen bottles of liquor.

At the sudden appearance of the officer, the three men jumped up and scrambled for an escape. Patrolman Pillars managed to grab the man he'd seen at McIntyre's Saloon and arrested him on charges of burglary and larceny. The other two men escaped.

Word had it that the three-story brick house the thieves had been hiding out in was known locally as the haunted house, though no specifics are given regarding its paranormal activity or why it may have earned this reputation. As often is the case, a glance back might speak on its character.

The house at 48 Main Street, which sat on the south side of the street between Sycamore and Elm Streets, was built about 1864 as a saloon and boardinghouse, with rooms to let on the two upper floors. The first saloon keeper was Elisha H. Roberts, who ran the place until around 1875, at which time, one James McDonald took over. Around 1881, the saloon started changing hands about every year or two, beginning with a man named William Kerrigan, followed in 1882 by Mrs. Bridget O'Rourke, during whose time the place almost burned down. James Barrett was next, followed by Thomas Moran and then finally Thomas F. Reilly, who was the last to operate the business. The building was vacated in 1887, and in time, it fell into disrepair and earned its haunted appearance and ghostly reputation.

It should be noted that the house seems to have had a colorful and, at times, relatively violent history. In 1878, a woman named Mary Ann Merrian was arrested for running a brothel out of the building. That same year, she was arrested for severely scalding a neighbor named Mrs. McGubron. In August 1882, a similar incident occurred when a woman named Bridget Carroll was taken into police custody and charged with assault for dumping boiling tea on a twelve-year-old girl named Julia McGrath. The following year, a sailor named Edward Carlin came home in a drunken rage and beat his wife senselessly. The judge who heard his case was so outraged that he wished to sentence the man to "the good old-fashioned whipping post," but as that was no longer legal, he fined the man and sentenced him to a month in the workhouse.

There were also at least a couple of deaths, if not more, that occurred in the place. The first of these occurred in 1883 with the death of Catherine

Main Avenue with the Harbor Inn in the foreground. *Photo by William G. Krejci.*

Killem, aged thirty-one years, who died from pneumonia. Three years later, saloon keeper Thomas F. Reilly died from an abscess at the age of twenty-five.

In 1900, the row of houses that made up the south side of Main Street, on the block between Elm and Sycamore Streets, was demolished to make way for an addition to the Cleveland Stove Company, later taken over by the Forest City Foundry.

One has to ask: What happens when you tear down the haunted house? Where do the spirits go? Some believe that they're set free and can finally move on, while others believe they continue to haunt the site. Yet there are a few, as we'll see later in chapter 23, who believe those ghosts simply take up residency in neighboring dwellings. Such may be the case here.

About one hundred feet away sits the Harbor Inn, which is famous in its own right, and as legend has it, it has a few ghost stories of its own. For several years now, bartenders have jokingly mentioned the ghosts of the Harbor Inn, but they won't exactly give specifics. Finally, after persistently bothering the staff, it was revealed that the ghostly activity appears to center on the stairwell that leads from the main barroom to the upstairs space. This usually comes in the form of the sound of footsteps ascending or descending the staircase. Some have also reported seeing moving figures in the gathered darkness and gloom of those upstairs rooms.

Of course, there's no way to know for certain who haunts a place or why, as there could be any number of reasons the Harbor Inn is haunted. In any case, it's a great place to sit back in the evening, raise some glasses and drink to the spirits of those who came before us—and may linger still.

16

A Haunting in Warrenton

40.189424, -80.679503

I was far too seriously startled by the suddenness with which this extraordinary apparition stood before me, in the dead of night and in that lonely place, to ask what she wanted.
—The Woman in White, *by Wilkie Collins*

Just north of the village of Rayland in Jefferson County on the Ohio River sat the small community of Warrenton. It was there, in May 1894, that a haunted house was causing quite a stir. It all goes back to the Higgins family, who were established in that community when Ohio was only a few years old.

Daniel Higgins Jr. was born in Washington County, Pennsylvania, in 1789. His father had served during the American Revolution and, in 1794, fought at the Battle of Fallen Timbers. In the first decade of the nineteenth century, the Higgins family came to Ohio and settled in Warren Township, Jefferson County. When the War of 1812 broke out, father and son both joined up to serve, the father as a private with the U.S. Infantry and the son as a sergeant with the Ohio Militia.

In 1818, Daniel Higgins Jr. married Elizabeth Revenaugh, with whom he'd have a daughter named Christina. Sadly, Elizabeth died just four years later. In 1824, he married his late wife's younger sister, Delilah Revenaugh, with whom he'd have seven more children. Daniel, who followed the trade of a carpenter since childhood, built a house in Warrenton on Broad Street, very close to the center of town. From there, he also operated a carpentry shop that was attached to their home. Daniel died on March 9, 1876, and was buried at nearby Warrenton Cemetery. His wife, Delilah, died on December 18, 1887, just one week after their daughter Theresa also passed.

Christina was married by that point and living in her own home. Daniel and Delilah's eldest living next of kin was their fifty-five-year-old daughter, Mary Jane Higgins, thus their house in Warrenton came into her possession. Unfortunately, as time passed, Mary Jane found that she was unable to keep up with paying the taxes on the property. The house went into foreclosure and was sold at sheriff's sale to a man named Christopher Vehrwoldt. At this, Mary Jane Higgins was evicted. Not long after, she took ill, and while lying on her death bed, she vowed that she would return from the spirit realm and haunt the house that was taken from her. She died soon after making that pledge.

Christopher Vehrwoldt rented the former Higgins house to Theodore Skaggs, who had grown up in Warrenton, just across the street from the Higgins family. Not long after moving in, the disturbances began. It seemed that Mary Jane Higgins was keeping her promise.

The story broke on May 7, 1894, that there was a haunted house in Warrenton, Jefferson County. It was reported that Theodore and Ella Skaggs, along with their children Maggie and Albert, were being terrified nightly by the spectral activity in their house. Every night since moving in, they had been awakened by rumbling noises that were described as sounding like someone pouring potatoes into an empty barrel. These sounds would occur about every five minutes for at least an hour, sometimes longer. The family would go through the house, night after night, searching for the source of the noise, but they came up with nothing.

Frank Linton, the village schoolteacher, thought that he would be able to solve the mystery of what was happening at the Skaggs home. He volunteered to sit in an upstairs room and wait for the activity to start. At around eleven o'clock that night, he heard the rumbling noise, which also rattled the windows. Mr. Linton and the family searched the house again in an attempt to find the source, but as before, they failed to do so. The disturbance carried on until around two o'clock in the morning, at which time it ceased.

It appears that the Skaggs family didn't remain long. By 1900, they were living in Stuebenville, about twelve miles north.

A terrible flood swept through Warrenton in March 1907, taking with it a number of homes, as well as the schoolhouse. The population started to drop off in the years that followed, and the village was ultimately

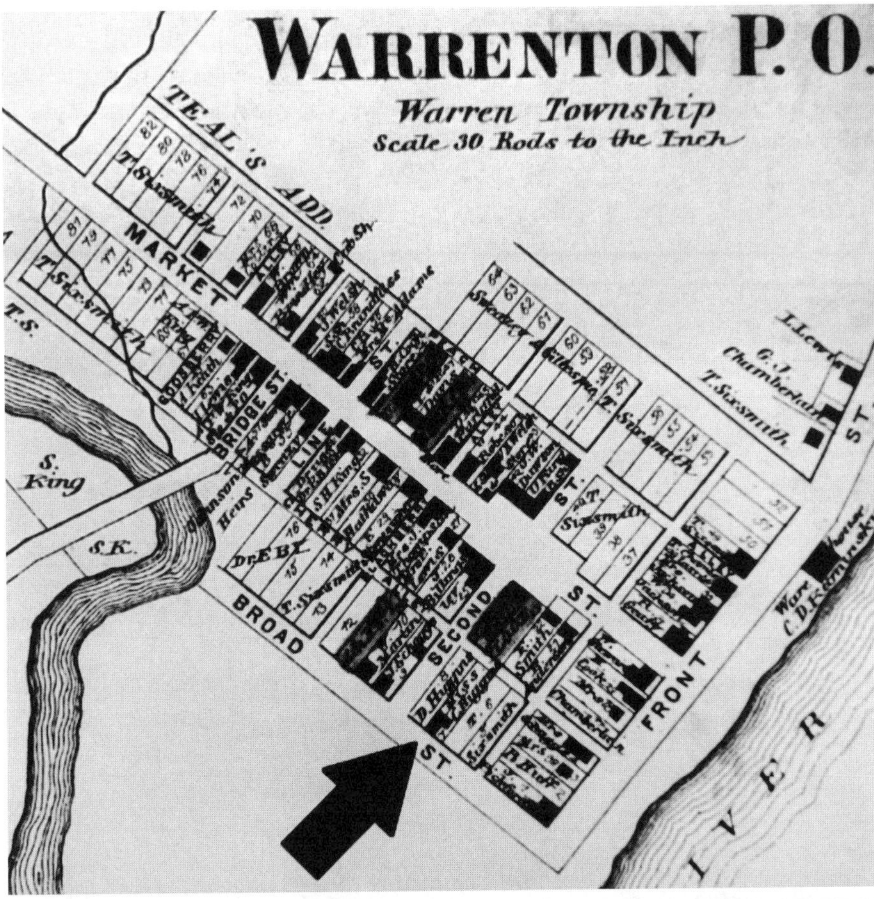

Top: A map showing the location of the Higgins House on Broad Street in Warrenton. *From* Atlas of Jefferson County, Ohio, *1871*.

Bottom: The former site of the Higgins House in Warrenton is today occupied by a gravel parking lot where boats are stored throughout the winter. *Photo by William G. Krejci*.

abandoned. Nearly every house has since been torn down, and hardly a trace remains today. The site of the old Higgins house is now part of a gravel lot, just within the entrance of the Short Creek boat launching area on County Road 17-A.

17

Their Marital Bed Is Haunted

41.481951, -81.701397

When by thy scorn, O murd'ress, I am dead
And that thou think'st thee free
From all solicitation from me,
Then shall my ghost come to thy bed
And thee, feign'd vestal, in worse arms shall see.
—"The Apparition," by John Donne

Pearl Street in Cleveland's west side Ohio City neighborhood is popular for its ghost stories. Tales are frequently told of the West Side Market, the old burying ground that once sat across the street from it and nearby Great Lakes Brewing, but it's the long-forgotten tales that we're here to rediscover. We've learned about the strange summoning in Mrs. Marquette's apartment by Dr. Rothermel and are about to hear of another location. This next story takes place in the apartment occupied by a liveryman and his wife. You'll read about a third haunting in chapter 21.

Concerning the livery:

Captain Rufus Curtis Sproul was born in Windsor, Maine, in 1821 but was raised out on the ocean. At the age of eleven, he started sailing on whaling vessels. In 1845, he moved to Cleveland but continued his sailing career on the Great Lakes, where he ultimately became a ship's captain. In 1852, he was married to Lydia M. Blake in Cleveland, and with her, he raised seven children.

Seeking a rest from the water, Rufus Sproul established his livery stable at 685 Pearl Street, where he also offered boarding stables and rented carriages for all purposes. He would enjoy his venture for only a few years, as he died on February 7, 1878, from heart disease and was laid to rest at nearby Monroe Street Cemetery. His wife, Lydia, continued to operate their business on Pearl Street as the Mrs. R.C. Sproul Livery.

The building that housed this business was a two-story frame structure, painted white, located near the manufacturing facilities of the Charles Rauch Carriage Works, later the Rauch and Lang Carriage Company. The first floor housed the livery, while the Sproul family resided in the apartments upstairs at 689 Pearl Street.

As the years passed, a number of Rufus and Lydia's children married and moved on, though a few remained at home. One of these children was Charles Baker Sproul, who was born in 1863. Charles continued in the family business as manager, overseeing many of the day-to-day operations of the livery. In May 1895, he married Harriett "Hattie" Foster, and the two moved into a second-floor apartment at 706 Pearl Street, located on the southeast corner of Pearl and Willey Streets, just to the south and across from the livery. The stage was set for marital bliss—with one exception. There was something terribly amiss with their bed.

That October, an incredible story emerged regarding the curious activity that was occurring in Charles and Hattie Sproul's apartment on Pearl. It was claimed by Charles Sproul that their bed was haunted, that it would pitch and toss about at night as though it was a ship in rough weather. Several nights earlier, he had retired to bed, and shortly after, the bed began to move of its own accord. One of the stablemen who worked at Sproul's livery verified the story, stating that the bed bucked about as though it was being tossed in a heavy sea.

The following night, two friends, Harry Underhill and James McGorray, having heard what was occurring, paid a visit to the Sprouls. Underhill said that if the bed was misbehaving, he'd like to see it for himself. He and James McGorray were shown into the bedroom, where they stretched themselves out on the bed and got comfortable. Within two or three minutes, the bed began to move about violently. McGorray jumped off immediately and ran out of the room, but Underhill and Sproul remained on the bed for a few more minutes, trying to puzzle out the cause. They investigated the matter by moving the bed into the middle of the room. Still, it did not cease in its movements. The men dismantled the bed and reassembled it, yet it continued to move about when anyone attempted to sit on it. Eventually, the

Sproul's Livery was the smaller white building immediately to the right of the Rauch and Lang Carriage Factory. *Library of Congress.*

shaking stopped, and the Sprouls were able to go to sleep that night. The following night, a Sunday, the bed was quiet and still, but on Monday and Tuesday, the gyrating resumed.

Charles Sproul stated that he'd purchased the bed, which was made of heavy oak, only ten months earlier. No one had ever died in it, and the only people who'd slept in it were he and his wife. He stated that he was in no way spiritualistic and was baffled as to the cause of the phenomenon. The owner of the building in which they resided, however, was extremely spiritualistic. George Ingham, who kept a store on the first floor, was one of the organizers of the West Side Progressive Lyceum, a spiritualistic organization that was founded around 1884.

IN HIS BED.

Charles Sproul Thinks a Ghost is After Him.

His Repose Disturbed by Strange Movements of His Couch—A Practical Joke Suspected.

Left: An article announces that Charles Sproul is haunted by a ghost "In His Bed." *From the* Cleveland Leader, *October 23, 1895.*

Below: The home of Charles and Hattie Sproul at 706 Pearl Street, Cleveland, circa 1922. *From the Cleveland Union Terminal Collection, the Michael Schwartz Library Special Collections, Cleveland State University.*

Mr. Ingham had suggested to the Sprouls that they attempt communication with whatever spirit might be influencing their bed. He proposed to them that they ask the spirit questions and tell it to reply numerically, in such a way that the number of shakes would equal the position of a letter as it appears in the alphabetic sequence. Charles Sproul said that they would not be doing that.

The paranormal activity wasn't confined to just Charles and Hattie Sproul's apartment. An elderly lady named Sarah E. Caldwell, who occupied another apartment on the second floor of the building, moved out abruptly after witnessing, on several occasions, her bedroom door, which was firmly bolted each night, unlock itself and swing open. The next morning, she'd find it closed again and secured, just as she'd left it the night before.

Within a few days, the Sprouls were growing weary of the publicity they were receiving regarding their unusual bed. Stories were becoming so exaggerated that people were claiming the windows in their apartment were flying open, and the bed was getting up and dancing around the room, concluding its performance by doing a full somersault. Many people were bothering them at all hours, asking to see the spirits in their bedroom. One intoxicated man showed up at their door late one night and offered to slay the ghost. Charles Sproul now went on record, contradicting previous statements and firsthand witness accounts, saying that he didn't know if the bed had really moved at all.

As Charles Sproul believed, no one had died in his bed. But what about his apartment?

Only one death at that location could be found. On Friday, June 20, 1890, Harriett Elizabeth "Hattie" Meech, aged forty-one years, died from spinal disease. Her funeral was held at the residence, and she was laid to rest at Monroe Street Cemetery.

As previously mentioned, the building's owner, George Ingham, was a noted spiritualist and one of the founders of the West Side Progressive Lyceum. At the group's establishment, the organizers placed one Althadine Smith in charge. Mrs. Smith had arrived in Cleveland from Oswego, New York, two years earlier. She was a very accomplished medium in her own right and was fast to make friends. Before long, it was learned that she'd come to Cleveland to get away from her abusive husband, who was a sailor on the Great Lakes. He'd twice previously sold all of their furniture, so upon her arrival in Cleveland, she purchased her own furniture with her own money. In time, her husband, Alfred, found her and again took up residency with her.

By early 1886, she'd had enough of his drinking and abuse. She had a friend, Louisa Jane Wilson, join her for support on the night of January 31 so that she could break it to her husband that they were over. The breakup went horribly wrong, and the bodies of Althadine Smith and Louisa Jane Wilson were discovered the following morning. Their cause of death was trauma to the head, inflicted by a claw hammer. Alfred Smith was arrested, tried and convicted of second-degree murder. He was sentenced to life in prison and died while incarcerated in 1898.

After the bodies of the two women were embalmed and dressed, they were placed in solid black coffins and put on display at William Heffron's undertakers' parlor so that everyone could see what their murderer had done. The following day, their remains were brought to George

Ingham's store at 706 Pearl Street, where they were again displayed before their funerals.

Whether any of this is accountable for the ghostly activity reported on the second floor of that building is anyone's guess.

It's unknown what, if anything, became of the bed. Perhaps the Sprouls continued to use it, in spite of its curious antics, or perhaps they parted with it altogether. Charles and Hattie Sproul continued to live at their apartment on Pearl Street until around 1903, at which time they moved to Willson Avenue, renamed East 55th Street, in 1906. Charles B. Sproul died on March 12, 1907, at the age of forty-three from tuberculosis and was laid to rest beside his family at Monroe Street Cemetery. Hattie died just three years later from dementia but was buried at Riverside Cemetery. She was only forty-two.

As for the house where the Sprouls' bed exhibited a ghostly personality, the address was changed in 1906 to 2191 West 25th Street. It was demolished in November 1925 to make way for a railroad line leading to the new Union Terminal, today the RTA Red Line.

18

THE RAVENNA HORROR

41.163301, -81.251460

There is danger overhanging, somewhere on the line. Some dreadful calamity will happen. It is not to be doubted this third time, after what has gone before. But surely this is a cruel haunting of me.
—*"The Signal-Man," by Charles Dickens*

On January 21, 1896, a flagman named William H. Rowley, while working on the New York, Lake Erie, & Western Railroad, more commonly known as the Erie Road, was knocked senseless by the water crane at the Ravenna Station as the train on which he was riding passed through the area at twenty-five miles per hour. Having been thrown from the train, he was severely injured yet miraculously escaped death. Ironically, Rowley had been the head brakeman on one of the two trains involved in what became known as the Ravenna Horror, one of the worst train wrecks in Ohio history. He'd survived the wreck but was reported among those injured. Curiously, the scene of his recent injury was the exact spot where the Ravenna Horror had occurred in 1891. According to reports in the newspapers, many of the men who worked the railroad in that area believed the site was haunted.

The Ravenna Horror was named so for good reason.

On July 3, 1891, at about 2:32 a.m., the No. 8, a first-class passenger train of eight cars and a locomotive, pulled into the station at Ravenna, having departed Kent almost twenty minutes earlier. Once the train came to a stop, the engineer took a couple of minutes to work on repairing his whistle, which had stopped working. Passengers were embarking and disembarking, just as they normally would. Dozing in the last car were a number of glass workers from Corning, New York, who were returning home from a convention in Findlay. None of them had any idea that the car they were resting in was about to become a hellish inferno.

Following just a few minutes behind the passenger train was the No. 82, a fast-moving freight train bound to New York from Chicago, pulling twenty-four cars heavily loaded with beef. Knowing that there was another train following them closely, the flagman from No. 8 ran down the tracks toward the approaching No. 82 in an attempt to raise a warning that they were still stopped at the station ahead, but it was all in vain. By the time the engineer saw him, it was too late.

A moment later, the light of the fast-approaching No. 82 flashed from around the bend at Morgan's Curve. The air was rent with the piercing sound of squealing brakes and then a terrible crash as the locomotive of the No. 82 telescoped into the rear car of the stopped No. 8 at thirty miles per hour, crushing a number of people to death in an instant.

All was quiet for only a moment, and then the moans of those trapped could be heard from within the wreckage. Within a minute, fire broke out in the rear car and quickly spread to the next two, where passengers had been sleeping. As those cars became engulfed in flames, the moans turned to screams. Many who lived in the area came running out of their houses to assist where they could. It was said that a woman and her child, trapped in the wreckage, were seen to catch fire and burn to death right in front of those who were attempting to rescue them.

In the end, at least nineteen people were dead, possibly more. It was hard to tell, as most of the remains were cremated beyond recognition. Of the group of glass workers from New York, eighteen of their party were listed among the dead. A monument now stands in their honor at St. Mary's Cemetery in South Corning.

After a thorough investigation, it was determined that the accident was caused by the two trains traveling too closely together, having an interval of only about four minutes between them. There were other factors, of course. The flagman of the No. 8 failed to set a fusee, or railroad flare, to indicate that a train was stopped ahead. Also, the engineer of the No. 82 was traveling at too great a speed and failed to blow his whistle as he approached the station. The worst of it was that the entire calamity could have been avoided if the cars of the No. 82 freight were equipped with air brakes. But they weren't.

HORRIBLE REAR END COLLISION ON THE ERIE ROAD AT RAVENNA, OHIO.

The scene of the Ravenna Horror. *From the* Saturday Globe *(Utica, NY), July 11, 1891.*

So, there you have it. The Ravenna Horror. It's hard to imagine a more appropriate name for a nightmarish catastrophe. Many believe that tragedies tend to affect a site and leave an impression. Is the location of the Ravenna Horror haunted, as trainmen who worked the railroad in that area believed? Possibly. Has that stretch of the Erie Road had a run of bad luck since then? Most certainly.

Exactly two months to the day after the Ravenna Horror, Lewis E. Jennings, an elderly gentleman and early settler of Ravenna, was struck by a train on the Erie Road. He survived the accident and was carried home to recover, though he never did so fully. Mr. Jennings hung on for an astonishing three years before he finally succumbed to his injuries. He died on Friday, October 26, 1894, and was laid to rest at Maple Grove Cemetery in Ravenna.

Lewis Jennings's death was followed two days later by that of another victim of the Erie Road. Edward Fahey, aged sixty-three, had escorted a friend that evening to the depot in Ravenna, and on his way home, he noticed a discarded railroad tie lying at the side of the tracks. He hurried home and returned with a wheelbarrow, which he left near the Chestnut Street crossing. He walked over to the tie, lifted it up and set it onto the tracks; then

A present-day view of the scene of the Ravenna Horror. *Photo by William G. Krejci.*

he started back to the Chestnut Street crossing to retrieve the wheelbarrow, which he'd apparently planned to use to cart the tie home. Just then, he must have heard the approaching train and, fearing the obstruction might cause a wreck, raced back to remove the tie from the tracks. He managed to lift it just in time but was then suddenly struck by the No. 90 Express, which killed him instantly.

On Sunday, May 29, 1910, Samuel and Mary Barr were returning from Maple Grove Cemetery, where they had gone to place flowers on the grave of their daughter, Minnie, who had died in 1903. On their way home, while crossing the Erie Road at Chestnut Street, the automobile they were driving was struck by the fast-moving Wells Fargo Express. There was no crossing gate, and Mr. Barr, it is assumed, misjudged the distance or speed of the train. The impact dragged their car more than one thousand feet from the point of impact. They were laid to rest beside their daughter two days later.

It should also be noted that only two months after the Ravenna Horror, three days before Lewis E. Jennings was stuck and critically injured, another collision took place on the line from Kent to Ravenna when two trains hit head-on, killing at least three and injuring more than two dozen. The cause of that wreck was a miscommunication in departure instructions on the part of the westbound freight, which left Ravenna early, not knowing that another train was coming and that the line was not clear.

Many years have passed since these horrific accidents occurred. The tracks of the Erie Road still exist and are paralleled by the Portage Hike and Bike Trail. The exact site of the Ravenna Horror—and the widely believed haunting that followed—lies on the tracks, across from a thicket of trees, between the Cleveland Road and North Diamond Street crossings.

19
Mrs. Matisofski's Spirit

And the Moon that night,
With a grey, cold light
Each baleful object tips;
One half of her form,
Is seen through the storm,
The other half's hid in Eclipse!
—*"The Hand of Glory," by Richard Harris Barham*

This next ghostly tale was passed along to me by Gavin Esposito, who possesses an incredible talent for historic research. He stumbled on this gem while doing a newspaper search on ghosts. The story returns us to the blue-collar industrial community of Hazelton on the edge of Youngstown, where the story of a haunted saloon was previously shared in chapter 8.

To tell this tale properly, we have to go back to November 22, 1895, when the family of E.H. Jones was living in Struthers, just south of Youngstown. It was there where Mr. Jones was engaged in work as an engineer at the Struthers Furnace. After finishing his shift at the furnace that morning, he came home to find his wife and three children unconscious. He immediately ran to their aid but was himself overcome and suddenly collapsed. A neighbor, in seeing this, pulled the family from the home.

As it turned out, the house was built on an old cinders dump for the furnace, and deadly gas had managed to seep out of the ground and into the house. Whether the gas actually came from the cinders or from the nearby furnace was never concluded. The family was revived, except for their one-year-old son, who died from the effects of the gas.

Less than a month earlier, a man named Nicholas Smith, who'd been employed at the Struthers Furnace for only three days, was asphyxiated by gas while cleaning the boilers. He'd been in the boiler for only a short time when he was overcome and collapsed. He died about an hour after he was pulled out.

Not long after the terrible incident with the Jones family, occupancy of the house was taken up by Joseph and Maria Matisofski.

Joseph had come to the United States from present-day Czechia, or the Czech Republic, then part of the Austro-Hungarian Empire. He settled in Hazelton, where he met Maria Jasecko, who also hailed from Czechia. The two were wed on May 11, 1892, and had one child, a son, whom they named Joseph.

In 1896, Joseph Matisofski took a job as a laborer at the Struthers Furnace and moved his family there from Hazelton, where his wife's family was located. They moved into the company house, which was formerly occupied by the Jones family, and took on seven other employees of the furnace as boarders.

On December 31, 1896, the family was celebrating the final hours of the year with four of their boarders, who were off for the night. Mrs. Matisofski was expecting their second child and wasn't feeling well. Her husband hadn't gone to work that evening and had instead stayed home with her on account of this. The doctor stopped by that night to check on her and noticed the house was closed up tight. He had them open a few of the windows to get some ventilation into the house. After he left, the windows were closed up again.

Around ten o'clock that night, the celebration dwindled, and everyone retired to bed. Three would never awaken.

At six o'clock the following morning, the other three employees who boarded there returned home from work at the furnace, ready for bed. They thought to wish their landlord and his family a happy new year and knocked on the Matisofskis' bedroom door, which was located on the first floor at the front of the house. There was no answer. They knocked again and called out, but still nothing. At this, they forced the door open and were met with a horrific scene. Gas had again filled the house, and death had carried away the lives of the entire Matisofski family. The three of them were lying close together on their bed. The other four boarders were found in their

The Matisofski monument at Calvary Cemetery in Youngstown. *Photo by William G. Krejci.*

rooms upstairs in a comatose state. They were quickly carried outside and eventually recovered.

The furnace company, which owned the house, believed the family were asphyxiated by a faulty cooking stove, not by gas that had come into the house from the nearby furnace. The origin of the deadly fumes was never determined.

The bodies of Joseph and Maria Matisofski and their two-year-old son were brought back to Maria's brother's house in Hazelton for burial. The funeral was held at the home a day later, and the three were laid to rest in section 3, lot 168 at Calvary Cemetery in Youngstown.

One thing that has been a constant in researching stories from the nineteenth century is this: newspapers have a habit of getting names wrong. This appears to have been the case here as well. The Matisofski family was incorrectly named in the papers as being the family of Joseph Betz (which also appears as "Bets" and "Best"). They also name Mrs. Matisofski's brother as being Joseph Tom. His name was, in fact, Michael Joseph Jasecko. At least they were close in properly spelling the name Matisofski when they reported on the haunting that followed a few weeks later.

It started shortly after the family was laid to rest. Strange noises started to echo through Maria's brother's house at night, and on several occasions, his wife thought that she'd seen the spirit of Mrs. Matisofski. This went on for quite a while, and in time, a number of the neighbors also claimed they witnessed apparitions about the place. Some even claimed they saw Mr. Matisofski and their young son.

The Jaseckos owned their house, but after experiencing the unexplainable phenomenon, they opted to move out and take up residency in an Andrews Bros. Company House on Edgewood Street, where they would have to pay rent. They had purchased their house less than a year earlier but preferred to let it stand vacant than stay in it another night. Ultimately, they found a tenant in a man named Joe Stone, who rented the home at a much-reduced rate. Mr. Stone didn't put much stock in ghost stories and didn't report any activity, but whatever had been happening in that house, it was enough to drive the Jaseckos out of their own home.

As you may have noticed, there are no GPS coordinates to accompany this story. The location of the Hazelton house that was said to be haunted by Mrs. Matisofski and, according to neighbors, her husband and son remains a mystery. Perhaps others know its location—or will discover it on their own someday.

20

The Empty Lot

41.504043, -81.655728

And often I so abhor this lonely lot
That my sick spirit a keen delight would take
In seeing some white ghost haunt some dusky spot,
Or setting a naked foot on some cold snake!
—*"The Atonement," by Edgar Fawcett*

On October 13, 1897, the *Cleveland Press* reported on an empty lot along lavish Euclid Avenue that was believed by many to be haunted. The lot, which was located near the intersection of Kennard Street, now East 46th Street, was set among the finest residential showpieces the Midwest had to offer, yet no house had ever been built on it. Most believed that this had something to do with the lot's storied history and haunted reputation.

The story of the lot was shared by someone simply identified as a prominent Cleveland lawyer. This anonymous source explained that about twenty years earlier, there was a young man from a very respectable family who resided in that part of town. Unfortunately, the young man was of very loose morals. He drank often and to excess and associated with a crowd of questionable character.

At some point, this man became acquainted with a young lady who worked as a domestic servant in the nearby home of another well-to-do family along Euclid Avenue's Millionaire's Row. He showed her much attention, and it seems the interest was returned. One evening, after he had imbibed more

An illustration of the haunted lot on Euclid Avenue. *From the* Cleveland Press, *October 13, 1897.*

alcohol than he could handle, he met with this young lady, and the two took a stroll to the vacant lot.

What happened next, no one could know for certain, but it was said that the two exchanged harsh words and a struggle ensued. The woman screamed, and the man grabbed her by the neck until she grew quiet and limp. Removing his hands from her throat, he soon realized that she was dead. He sobered up instantly in the shock of the moment, knowing that he had just become a murderer.

It's said that he quickly removed the young woman's garters and tied them together. He then slipped them around her neck and somehow managed to lift her body high enough to fasten the other end around a low-lying limb on the nearest tree. There, he left her body to hang through the rest of the night.

The following morning, the body of the unfortunate girl was discovered hanging from the tree. As there appeared to be no sign of a murder, her cause of death was ruled to be suicide. But from that day on, as buildings and fine homes were erected around the fatal site, no structure was placed there.

The realization of the man's awful secret grew heavier and heavier on his conscience until he could stand it no longer. He sought out an elderly attorney he'd known for some time and shared the story of what had happened without the slightest hint of restraint. The attorney advised him to keep quiet on the matter and said no one would ever be the wiser. That was the course that was taken. According to the teller of this story, both the young man and the elderly attorney had since died.

As the years passed, people came to regard the empty lot with a feeling of fear, and in time, many believed the site was haunted. Children dreaded the place, and anyone who heard the story would cross the street when passing the site after nightfall.

In the years that followed the publication of this story, the empty lot on Euclid Avenue, which had been owned by business and civic leader Jacob Bishop Perkins, remained empty, at least until 1904. It was then that the magnificent Euclid Avenue Garden Theater was built on the site. The entrance gatehouse for this establishment, built with a strong Spanish influence, was set back two hundred feet from the road. Beyond the gatehouse were the beautifully laid-out gardens. The theater itself, which was at the back of the property, accommodated 1,500 people. The main entrance was reached by a large horseshoe drive. It was used primarily as a summer venue for comic opera and vaudeville performances, but it could be closed up to accommodate performances during wet or chilly weather.

Sadly, the Euclid Avenue Garden Theater was a relatively short-lived venture. The property was sold in November 1911 to the Standard Sanitary Manufacturing Company of Pittsburgh, and the theater was demolished the following year to make way for a massive warehouse, which still stands on the western part of the lot. The eastern half is occupied by a driveway entrance to two parking lots.

21
Elizabeth Rafferty's Ghost

41.486457, -81.704944

Be silent in that solitude,
Which is not loneliness—for then
The spirits of the dead who stood
In life before thee are again
In death around thee—and their will
Shall overshadow thee: be still.
—*"Spirits of the Dead," by Edgar Allan Poe*

By 1901, John and Elizabeth Rafferty had been married for eleven years. Elizabeth, or Lizzie, as she sometimes preferred, was born in Canada in May 1853. Her parents originally hailed from Pennsylvania. Meanwhile, her husband, John, was a native of New York and worked as a captain on a Great Lakes steamer, which kept him away from home for most of the year.

The Raffertys, who had no children, lived at various locations around Cleveland until around 1900, when Elizabeth opened a restaurant at 452 Pearl Street. She lived that year just a few doors south, but in 1901, she took up residency in an apartment on the second floor of a frame building at 486 Pearl Street. While living there, she would receive the fright of her life.

Mrs. Rafferty flat out insisted that she never believed in ghosts, yet she was unable to explain the phenomenon that had been worrying her to the extent that she was unable to sleep at night. In the darkness, her house would fill with ear-piercing whistling sounds, groans and a loud rattle that shook the place. One night before bed, she put her dog out into the hall but awoke in the middle of the night to find him sitting on the floor in the middle of the room, chewing on a bone. Unable to understand how the dog had gotten back in, she climbed out of bed to let him out again, but when she reached him, he vanished. She went to the door to look down the hall but turned around for just a moment to see the dog again, sitting in the middle of the room. At this, she opened the door to the hall and looked out. There, she saw her dog fast asleep on the hallway floor. She turned again to look back into her room, and the same dog was sitting behind her, still chewing on that bone. She couldn't understand how the same dog could be in two places at the same time.

The mysterious activity also occurred in daylight. There was a certain ornament that Mrs. Rafferty kept pinned to a trunk. On one occasion, she left the room for a moment, and when she returned, the ornament was pinned to the floor. She returned it to the trunk, but every time she did so and left the room, she returned to find it in a completely different location. Mrs. Rafferty also had a certain drinking glass that she'd once placed on the mantle and then left the room. When she came back, the glass was on the floor with a number of other items piled up on top of it. When she picked it up and returned it to the mantle again, it began to shake. The glass must have been in the apartment when she moved in. She'd been told that a man who had previously occupied that apartment died by suicide after drinking poison from that glass. She accepted that as the reason why the glass wouldn't stay still.

Many of her neighbors had heard the stories but had their doubts. She challenged them to investigate the matter for themselves, and it was said that many of them witnessed the same phenomenon. Between the antics of the drinking glass, her ornament being moved around and the sudden appearance of the phantom dog, not to mention all of the nightly noises, Elizabeth Rafferty was reaching the end of her tether. Hearing about the death by suicide seemed to be the last straw for her.

Mrs. Rafferty was acquainted with a man who claimed to be a ghost charmer of sorts. He asserted that he had the ability to exercise control over the weird and invisible mischief makers of the night. She believed that he might be her only option at that point. She sent for him, but before he arrived, she suddenly heard her room fill with the voices of a chorus singing a funeral dirge.

Upon his arrival, the ghost charmer started to wander the room, mumbling strange words and whispering incantations. He then handed Mrs. Rafferty

A view of 1817 West 25th Street in 1954, formerly the location of the house at 486 Pearl Street, where Mrs. Rafferty lived. At the time, the first floor of the building was occupied by a leather shop. Today, the site is occupied by Riverview Tower. *Photo courtesy of the Cleveland Public Library Photograph Collection.*

a small roll of yellow paper and told her to display it in the house. If she did this, the ghosts would seek safety elsewhere. She did as she was told and displayed the paper in a conspicuous place, though it's not clear if she simply set the roll down somewhere or unrolled it and hung it up about the place. Either way, it seemed to work. In time, Elizabeth Rafferty was no longer troubled by spirits from the world beyond.

Still, the Raffertys didn't remain at that address very long. In a short time, they moved to a house on Wentworth Avenue, but a few years later, they moved to Conneaut, where John was put in charge of the harbor tugboats.

Are you troubled by strange noises in the middle of the night? Do you experience feelings of dread in your basement or attic? Have you or any of your family ever seen a spook, specter or ghost? Have you witnessed a large phantom dog chewing on a bone in the middle of your bedroom? If the answer is yes, then you may need to call—well—someone. But before you seek the expert assistance of a local ghost charmer or otherwise, you just might want to consider trying the small roll of yellow paper solution. You never know. It may just do the trick.

22
THE KENASTON FARMHOUSE

41.326309, -82.256842

The phantom shapes, which were becoming gradually materialized from the moonbeams, were those of the three ghostly women to whom I was doomed.
—Dracula, *by Bram Stoker*

As you may have noticed by now, the stories in this book are being told chronologically. Therefore, it is purely by coincidence that the next three accounts all took place in Lorain County—they also happen to be the only stories from Lorain County found in these pages. The first of these stories was reported in 1901 in Russia Township, just northwest of Oberlin.

Professor Carlos Alfred Kenaston was born on April 12, 1838, in Sherbrooke, Quebec, to parents David and Sarah Kenaston. In 1842, he moved with his family to Oberlin, where he spent his most formative years. At the age of fifteen, he began his studies at Oberlin College, and in 1861, he received his bachelor's degree. The following year, he married Lucy Kellogg Fairchild, the daughter of Oberlin College President James Fairchild. Two years later, Carlos Kenaston earned his master's degree.

Much of his career was spent in academics, as he taught at a number of schools and universities, including Salt Lake College, Howard University and the Agriculture College in Lansing, Michigan, which soon after became Michigan State University. He left academia for a time to work as a civil engineer on various railroads and even served in government with the Treasury Department and the Department of the Interior.

A portrait of Carlos Alfred Kenaston. *Photo courtesy the Oberlin College Archives.*

He ultimately retired from government and scholarly pursuits in 1897 and returned to Oberlin. Originally residing with Lucy's widowed father, Carlos and Lucy Kenaston sought a quiet life outside of town. In 1900, they purchased a rundown house, which sat on a one-hundred-acre tract, that being the southern portion of lot 32 in Russia Township.

Standing on the east side of what was then known as Gaston Road, the little farmhouse dated to at least the early 1840s, if not slightly earlier. It was built by a man named Heman Gaston, who had come to Russia Township from Berkshire, Massachusetts, with his family in 1838. Just after Gaston's arrival with his family, his wife, Mary, passed away. Heman Gaston followed her to the grave in 1855. The farm then came into the hands of his nephew, Alonzo Gaston, who died in 1892. From there, it passed to his daughter, Ameilia Rebecca Gaston, who sold the farm to the Kenastons.

Now, it should be pointed out that Carlos Kenaston had two brothers, Herbert, who was killed in action at Gettysburg in 1863, and Arthur, who was something of an eccentric. Arthur was a student of the occult sciences but worked as a painter and a litigation attorney. He was notorious for using extreme measures to prove his case. Upon the death of his mother in 1895, he refused to pay for her coffin, claiming that it was not what he had ordered from the undertakers. Five years later, the undertakers brought a suit against him for the cost of the coffin. To prove that it wasn't what he had ordered, Arthur Kenaston dug up his mother's grave and removed a piece of the coffin, which he produced in court. As Kenaston had made his case, the undertakers now admitted that the coffin wasn't exactly what he had ordered. Still, the jury sided with the undertakers, stating that they would never favor a man who would unearth and cut up his own mother's coffin.

Apparently, it was well noted in the area of Oberlin that the house Carlos and Lucy Kenaston had just purchased from the Gaston family was haunted. Those who knew the stories would pass the house at a run and wouldn't stop until they were well away from it and out of breath. Weird tales had been told of dark and bloody crimes that had been committed in the house, of ghosts that would glide through the glancing beams of moonlight and of screams and wails that would cause one's hair to stand on end and the blood in their veins to run cold.

It was also said that the Gaston family, who did not occupy the house in later years, had sought a tenant for the last two decades. One man, some years earlier, had scoffed at the ghostly tales that were told about the house and was induced to take up residency. A single night was enough. The stories he told the next day only added to the superstitious awe in which the place was held.

Lucy and Carlos Kenaston didn't put much stock in the ghost stories either. They believed that some repairs and a couple of coats of paint might drive away any spirits that lingered about the house—or at least drive away the stories that were told about it.

About a year after purchasing the farmhouse, Professor Kenaston's brother Arthur shared an experience that he'd had late one night at the old haunted house. He was talking to a judge in Oberlin when he made the admission.

"For years," he began, "I have been a believer in occultism, and unconsciously, I have become an occultist. Often, I have tested my powers in this direction with astonishing results." In relation to his brother's house, he continued, "The other night, I went to bed, wondering if the stories that had been told about the place were true. In the middle of the night, I was awakened by a voice saying, 'Go and see.'"

He quietly arose and, without waking his wife, got dressed, went outside and slowly made his midnight journey to his brother's house. "When I arrived there," Arthur Kenaston continued, "I walked quietly around the house a couple of times and finally sat down on a ladder which was leaning against the rear of the house. It was a beautiful night. A soft breeze played

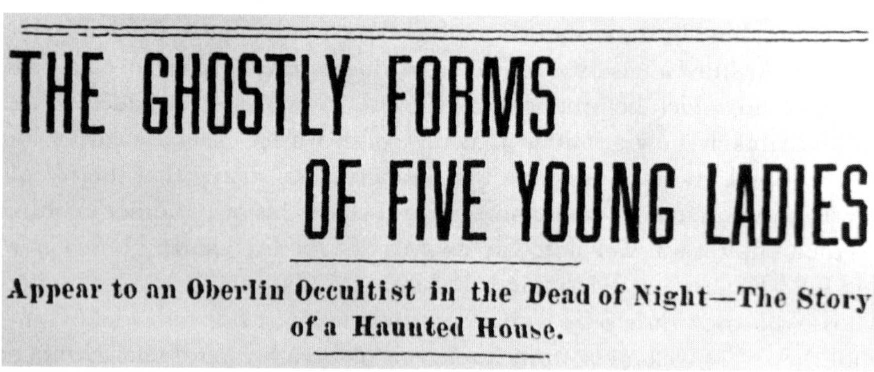
THE GHOSTLY FORMS OF FIVE YOUNG LADIES

Appear to an Oberlin Occultist in the Dead of Night—The Story of a Haunted House.

A headline announced the visitation of "The Ghostly Forms of Five Young Ladies" to Arthur Kenaston. *From* The Elyria Reporter, *July 3, 1901.*

The former Kenaston farmhouse on Quarry Road in Oberlin. *Photo courtesy the Lorain County Auditor's Office.*

among the leaves of the trees and the stars shone with an unusual brilliancy. As I sat there, I gradually went into a trance, and suddenly in the starlight I saw the form of a young lady approaching, and behind her came four other female forms. They were all dressed in white, and as they passed before me, each one stopped and faced me, and as they did so, each in turn raised her right hand with the index finger extended, and then, throwing back her head, she drew her finger across her throat and vanished into the night. I no longer have any doubts as to whether or not the house is haunted."

Thorough research into the history of the house has revealed nothing, certainly none of the crimes dark and bloody that neighbors had previously suggested. Still, there may have been something to what Arthur Kenaston witnessed that night. If it was not a shadow of the past, then perhaps he had received a warning of terrible things to come. The following year, Carlos Alfred Kenaston suffered a debilitating stroke that ultimately claimed his life in 1905. Arthur Kenaston died in 1903, just two years after the ghostly visitation.

The Kenaston farmhouse still stands at 11273 Quarry Road in Russia Township, Lorain County. To the best of this author's knowledge, the five phantom women have not been seen for 125 years.

23
The Ghost of Beebe's Tavern

41.367418, -82.100686

And who, most mysterious of all, was the fair-faced vision I beheld at the window? Or was it, as many believe, the specter of the tavern?
—The Black Mask, *by Annie Lydia Smith*

About a month after reports of the ghostly women at the Kenaston farmhouse began to circulate, so, too, did those of a phantom at the Cleveland, Elyria & Western Electric Railway trolley barns in Elyria. The barns were located on the south side of East Broad Street, just across from East Bridge Street.

For some time, peculiar noises had been heard about the place by men working in the barns late at night. They did their best not to discuss the matter, but as of late, the encounters were becoming more and more vivid. Late one night around mid-August 1901, a crew was bringing in their trolley when they suddenly saw a white-sheeted figure, believed to be a woman, enter the barn, walk the length of it and then suddenly vanish without a trace. A thorough search of the place was made, but nothing turned up. At this, the late-night crew came forward and shared their experiences with the heart-rending groans and wailings that took place nightly between eleven and three o'clock. A number of the men had considered submitting their resignations, while others were more committed to the idea of solving the mystery.

About a week and a half later, a young boy named Brown, who swept out the cars at night, witnessed the ghost as it appeared before him. He

A woodcut print of Beebe's Tavern in Elyria. *From* History of Lorain County, Ohio, *1879.*

was paralyzed with fear and could hardly talk for about an hour. When he regained the power of speech, he vowed that he would never set foot in the car barns again. Many were beginning to believe that the phantom was either some poor soul who had escaped from hell or the victim of some terrible crime that had been committed many years ago in the vicinity of where the trolley barns now stood.

In early September, the employees of the CE&W Electric Railway came to the conclusion that the ghost haunting their trolley barn was actually, in some manner, connected with the old building located immediately next door to the west, that being the former Beebe's Tavern.

Born in Massachusetts on October 7, 1793, Artemas Beebe was one of a small party who accompanied Heman Ely, for whom Elyria was named, from West Springfield, Massachusetts, to Ohio in 1817. One year later, Beebe built his tavern on the south side of what would become Broad Street. As Heman Ely built his home directly across the road from Beebe's Tavern, many consider this location to be the birthplace of Elyria. Beebe's Tavern, being the first hotel in town, was, by default, the home of all newcomers until their own houses could be built. It was also where most social gatherings were held, including the first meeting of Elyria's original Masonic lodge. In later years, it was the main stagecoach stop on the road leading through town.

Artemas and Parmelia Beebe. *From* History of Lorain County, Ohio, *1879*.

In 1820, Artemas Beebe returned to West Springfield to marry Parmelia Morgan. They returned to Elyria later that year and raised a family. Beebe continued to operate the tavern until 1834, at which time, he rented out the concern and focused on other endeavors. In 1846, he built the Beebe Hotel, a four-story brick building, on the northwest corner of Elyria's Public Square. As for the old tavern stand, it continued to operate under the direction of two men named Byington and Mygatt until 1837, when S.W. Willard took over the operation.

Perhaps the name Beebe will sound familiar to some of my regular readers. One of Artemas and Parmelia's children, Henry Beebe, opened a fine hotel at Put-in-Bay in 1869 called the Beebe House. Considered one of the grandest hotels to grace the Lake Erie islands, the hotel sadly burned down in 1932. More on that story can be found in my book *Lost Put-in-Bay*.

As for the old tavern stand in Elyria, in time, it ceased being used as a hotel and was renovated into a private residence. It was said, however, that the first two families who occupied it for that purpose moved out rather abruptly shortly after moving in. This was on account of ghostly sounds and appearances, as well as the doors swinging open after they were securely locked. One unconfirmed claim asserted that a man was killed in the old

A present-day view of the former site of Beebe's Tavern in Elyria. *Photo by William G. Krejci.*

tavern in a quarrel over a card game. Many believed that his ghost continued to haunt Beebe's Tavern through some hard feeling he bore toward it.

When asked about the haunting of the former tavern, the Jackson brothers, meatpackers from Cleveland who owned it, claimed that they had no knowledge of its haunted reputation or of the stories that had been told about it.

Eventually, the house was renovated to accommodate many families, and through much of the first part of the twentieth century, it was used as an apartment building. By the late 1930s, the building had fallen into a state of neglect and was soon condemned by the Elyria fire chief. There was a movement to have the house relocated to the back of the property, renovated and converted into a history museum, but those plans ultimately fell through.

The former Beebe's Tavern, believed at the time to have been the oldest standing building in Lorain County, was demolished in August 1941. Today, the site is occupied by the parking lot immediately to the west of an auto service center at 100 East Broad Street. A state historical marker that speaks on the first settlement of Elyria is located directly across the street.

24
A Ghost in Marsh Kelley's House

But the country folks, if you asked them, would swear on their Bibles that he walks. There are those who speak to having met him near the church, and on the moor, and even within this house.
—Wuthering Heights, *by Emily Brontë*

Returning to Oberlin, we find the Kelley family residing in a home near the north end of town. The occupants at the time were Marshall "Marsh" Kelley; his wife, Sarah "Sadie" Adelia Denn-Kelley; and their two-year-old daughter, Vera. At the time, Sadie was expecting another child. Also residing with them was Sadie's brother, Albert Denn. Both Marsh and Albert worked together doing odd jobs around town.

For some time, the northern end of town had been quite excited over reports that there was a haunting occurring in the home of Marsh Kelley. The events seemed to peak on the night of August 19, 1904. At around one o'clock in the morning, the entire family was awakened to strange sounds coming from the first floor of the house. Marsh Kelley and his brother-in-law came down from their bedrooms on the second floor to investigate.

On reaching the first floor, they found every single door in the house open, and upon entering the sitting room, they were grabbed by a ghost that they claimed was over six feet tall and robed in white. Marsh Kelley was successful in getting out of the house and alerting his neighbors to what was transpiring. Meanwhile, his brother-in-law was so terribly frightened that he fainted on the spot. A thorough search of the house and property was made, but no further evidence could be gathered.

OBERLIN HAS A GHOST.

The Spook is Muscular, and a Crowd Has Been Organized to Waylay It.

A headline declaring that "Oberlin Has a Ghost." *From the* Plain Dealer, *August 21, 1904.*

In the end, it was decided that a group would get together the following evening and wait in the house for the ghost to return. As the trail goes dead and no further reports on the matter were made, it can be safe to assume that the ghost failed to appear.

It should be noted that when the story was first covered, Albert Denn chose to give his name as "A. Easterwood," using his mother's maiden name instead of giving his own surname.

By 1910, the Kelleys, as well as Albert Denn, were all living with Sadie's father, Henry Denn, at 163 North Pleasant Street in Oberlin. As this house is located in the same area indicated in the article, it may be that this was where the Kelley family was residing at the time of the haunting. Still, the article makes no mention of Sadie's father, so one cannot be certain based on the limited information that was made available.

Ultimately, the Kelleys moved to Painesville, where Marsh tragically died in 1917, following an accident that took off both of his legs. He was forty-one. Sadie died just five years later.

Again, very little information was given regarding the exact location of this haunting. Perhaps a reader would like to try their hand at cracking that mystery.

25

THE GHOSTS OF WHISKEY SPRING

40.247904, -81.629785

A hound it was, an enormous coal-black hound, but not such a hound as mortal eyes have ever seen. Fire burst from its open mouth, its eyes glowed with a smouldering glare, its muzzle and hackles and dewlap were outlined in flickering flame.
—The Hound of the Baskervilles, *by Sir Arthur Conan Doyle*

Flowing from under a rock at the side of a road in Oxford Township, Coshocton County, we find a spot called "Whiskey Spring," named by the old settlers of that area. A description from the *Coshocton Daily Age*, dated January 6, 1905, described it as being located beside the road leading from Low Gap to Newcomerstown and on the farm of the late Philip Loos. It received its unique name from certain circumstances and traditions that took place at the site.

Shortly after the completion of the Ohio and Erie Canal in 1832, Newcomerstown became a major market hub for the exportation of wheat. During the first week of October, countless wagons full of grain would pass along that road on their way to market. Farmers would usually arrive in town around ten or eleven o'clock in the morning and would commence unloading their product. Once the task was complete, they would procure a jug of whiskey to accompany them on the journey back home. Bringing feed for their horses and lunch for themselves, the farmers would usually stop at the roadside spring to feed and water their horses, eat their lunch, take a swig or two out of the jug of old rye and complete their trip home as happy as can be.

Curiously, there were also a number of ghost stories connected with Whiskey Spring. These were related by a man named James Magness. At the age of eighty-five, Mr. Magness, a retired farmer and schoolteacher, resided in nearby Plainfield, about five miles southwest of the storied site.

"There is an uncanny romance about this spring worth relating," Magness began.

> *It is said that the place was haunted. There is said to have been seen there at nights a very large mastiff dog, which was only an apparition. Also, a barrel was often seen rolling down the hill above the spring and crossing the road. This was supposed to be a barrel of whiskey. A headless cow was seen coming down the hill, probably on the hunt of the whiskey.*
>
> *The skeleton of a man was plowed up near the spring by David Marlatt of Marlatt's Run. This was supposed to be the skeleton of a pack peddler whose kit was found over in the woods behind the hill above the spring. This kit had been pillaged but no account of the peddler was ever given. It is supposed that the peddler was murdered and his body buried in the soft ground below the spring and only plow deep.*
>
> *The story is told that two boys were out hunting near the spring and their dog treed a groundhog up a sapling. The boys were trying to shake it down when it let go and fell on one of the boys and the dog and killed both.*

James Magness further explained that there were many more stories regarding the site and tragedies that had occurred there, but to share those would have made the article too long. Too long or not, it would have been wonderful if he'd have told them. He passed away five months later.

Fortunately, a couple of these stories were elaborated on when, eight years later, two old friends got together to reminisce. Festus "Fet" McCluskey, a prominent real estate dealer in Cuyahoga Falls, had been born and raised on what later became the Philip Loos farm. His father, Andrew McCluskey, had purchased that tract, forty acres, sometime around 1860 and had been the one who cleared the land for farming.

It was during a homecoming that Fet McCluskey got together with his boyhood friend James Haver. They were as familiar with the stories of Whiskey Spring as they were with every inch of their fathers' cabins. They recalled the headless cow that would make its nocturnal journeys down the steep hillside to drink at the spring, but how she managed to quench her thirst without a head, none could guess. They also recounted the tale of the giant shaggy ghost dog. It was said that an elderly woman who lived in

Above: Whiskey Spring still flows from the side of the road, running from Low Gap to Newcomerstown. *Photo by William G. Krejci.*

Right: James Magness. *Photo courtesy of Ashley Miller.*

the area would periodically make trips on horseback to Newcomerstown to procure tobacco, snuff or any other such necessities that her neighbors were in need of. She would often have strange adventures on her return journey after nightfall. If the night was dark, she was sure to meet the phantom dog just as she emerged from the Mulvane Ford. With one tremendous bound, the dog would leap on the horse's rump and hold on as the horse took off at a fast pace, riding unbidden behind the terrified woman. It would hang on past the spring, across the Low Gap Hill and down to Marlatt's Run beyond, where it would vanish.

Today, the sleepy little site comprises a few private residences set among the rolling hills, woods and fields of Coshocton County. Whiskey Spring, just as described by James Magness, still emerges from the earth beside the road from Low Gap to Newcomerstown. The area is beautiful and enchanting.

26
Meyers Lake

40.813499, -81.415129

It is said that the Spirits of buried men
Oft come to this wicked world again;
That the churchyard turf is often trod
By the unlaid tenants of tomb and sod,
That the midnight sea itself is swept,
By those who have long beneath it slept.
And they say of this old, mossy wood,
Whose hoary trunks have for ages stood,
That every knoll and dim-lit glade
Is haunted at night by its restless Shade.
—*"The Haunted Wood," by Isaac McLellan*

In August 1906, a man named Joe Riegler took a stroll with a reporter from the *Canton Repository* around Meyers Lake Park, just a couple miles northwest of downtown Canton. He recalled life from more than fifty years ago, back before there were any electric lights or electric streetcars. They strolled along the main thoroughfare, called The Pike, on which were set most of the amusements, rides and attractions.

The amusement park at Meyers Lake opened in 1880 on lands previously owned by Andrew Meyer. A boat club and a hotel were added as amenities, and an electric trolley line operated by the Northern Ohio Traction & Light Company serviced the resort. In time, a scenic railroad, roller coaster and water ride called the Rustic Mill were added.

A postcard shows The Pike at Meyers Lake in Canton. *Author's collection.*

"To walk to the lake," Joe explained, "we usually went by way of Phillips' lime quarry and then followed up the ravine. At that time, fishing was good, and it was no trick to land a fine catch. Only a few row boats were on the lake and a gasoline launch was unknown. In later years, a few small sailboats were added. The lake was not frequented in earlier days by pleasure seekers as it was by fisherman and hunters. The place used to be alive with wild ducks and wild geese, but few of them are to be seen around this locality now."

According to Joe Riegler, the lake was surrounded by timberlands, and that part of the grove, where The Pike was located, was more like a wilderness in the early years. "Many people were really afraid to penetrate the woodland in which we are at present," he continued. "It was always claimed that the woods were haunted, and some would not venture here day or night."

He didn't elaborate on any of the specifics regarding paranormal activity, nor did he give any reason about why the location would have been haunted. But he stated, "Quite a number of people have been drowned in this water during my recollection, and I helped to save the lives of a number while I was boat-tender."

It's true that Meyers Lake does have a long history of tragic deaths. Aside from the countless drownings—and there really are too many to count—there have been more than a few freak accidents at the park. In 1901, Jesse Hinder, age twelve of Massillon, was killed when he was struck in the head

Today, much of the site of The Pike at Meyers Lake is occupied by Harbor Drive. *Photo by William G. Krejci.*

by a water toboggan, which crushed his skull. The same happened to fifteen-year-old Elmer Ball of Canton on September 16, 1907. He died on an operating table two hours after the accident. Many believed it a miracle that he survived even that long.

The most horrific incident occurred on July 27, 1912, when an aeronaut named Thomas "Tommy" Heifield, age twenty-eight, was killed while performing an aerial trapeze stunt from a hot air balloon. He fell eight hundred feet to his death in front of a crowd of thousands of spectators.

Meyers Lake Amusement Park closed in 1974 and was developed into a residential community. Today, much of The Pike at Meyers Lake is occupied by the southwest end of Harbor Drive. The old, haunted woods in the grove have been replaced by modern homes.

27
Are These the Bones of Dan Blakeslee?

41.950415, -80.544064

I was haunted by those old bones for years; they used to come rattling after me into my great empty room, and shake themselves in my ears—nothing would shut them out.
—A Sprig of Heather, *by Geraldine Butt*

"Skeleton Is Clew to Crime."

So heads an article in the *Cleveland Press*, dated December 29, 1906. The article states that evidence of a mysterious murder, which explains a remarkable disappearance a quarter of a century earlier, was discovered that week in the unearthing of the skeleton of a man near the ruins of an old farmhouse. The skeleton was found buried close to the outside wall of what had formerly been the Nathaniel Harmon House in Conneaut, Ashtabula County. The gruesome discovery was made by hunters who stumbled on the remains and dug them up. They noticed at once that the skull had been crushed by some blunt object.

"This accounts for the disappearance of Dan Blakeslee, a smuggler, twenty-five years ago," said Alvin V. Van Gorder, an old neighbor of the Harmon family. "Blakeslee boarded with the Harmons. It was common report that he smuggled goods across the lake from Canada, and once he was chased by revenue officers.

"When Harmon and his wife died, Blakeslee continued to live with the son and two daughters. A love affair caused some trouble. One of the girls wanted to marry, and her brother objected. Blakeslee took the side of the girl."

Van Gorder explained that Blakeslee disappeared around that time, and not the slightest clue about what became of him was ever obtained. The article went on to claim that all the members of the Harmon family were now deceased and that the Harmon house had been torn down a year earlier, after having been unoccupied for more than a dozen years. Many women who lived in the vicinity insisted that the old house was haunted and that a ghostly figure was seen wandering the grounds at night.

One would think that the discovery of these remains would solve two mysteries: what happened to Dan Blakeslee and why the grounds of the Harmon house were haunted. Unfortunately, it turns out, this wasn't the case.

First, a little about the house.

Nathaniel Bridgeman Harmon was born on December 19, 1790, in New Marlborough, Massachusetts. Being one of the earliest settlers of that area, he was married to Sarah Parmely "Sally" Leet in Ashtabula in October 1814. Over the next fourteen years, Sally gave birth to no less than eight children, two of whom died in early childhood. The family resided in Ashtabula until 1825, when they briefly moved to Salem Township. They finally took up residency in Conneaut in 1833. Harmon built his farmhouse on the upper bank along the east side of Conneaut Creek, and there, he and his wife raised their family.

In 1850, Sally died and was laid to rest at the City Cemetery in Conneaut. Six years later, Nathaniel Harmon married again. His second wife was Sylvinia Thanksful Stockwell-Marks. They had one child, a son named Nathan B. Harmon Jr. Shortly after Nathan Jr.'s birth, Harmon moved with his wife and son to Kalamazoo, Michigan, at which time, his house in Conneaut was transferred to his daughter Lucinda, who occupied it with her sister Sarah until Sarah's death from typhoid fever in 1873. Four years later, Lucinda married a widower named David W. Gary and moved to Ashtabula. Meanwhile, her father, Sylvinia, and half brother moved back to Ohio but settled in Willoughby, Lake County, where Nathaniel Bridgeman Harmon Sr. died in 1881.

While it's true that Nathaniel Harmon Sr. and his second wife, Sylvinia, were both deceased at the time this article was written, Sylvinia having died in 1902, their son Nathaniel Jr. was still very much alive. In fact, he lived to the grand age of ninety-eight and died in 1955. He'd moved out to California immediately following the death of his father.

The old Harmon property was eventually sold to the Conneaut Land Company. The house sat derelict for a number of years before it was torn

A modern house crowns the former site of the Harmon House in Conneaut. *Photo courtesy of the Ashtabula County Auditor's Office.*

down in 1905. A second house, currently owned by the Bessemer & Lake Erie Railroad, was built on the site of the first house in 1915.

Curiously, in all this family history related to the Harmons, no evidence can be found regarding anyone named Dan Blakeslee living anywhere near Conneaut, let alone as a boarder with the Harmon family. It's true that there was a Blakeslee family in that town, but no records of a Dan Blakeslee could be located. What's more, there's little evidence to support the story that one of Harmon's daughters wished to marry but had a brother who violently objected. Perhaps Van Gorder was referring to Lucinda and Sarah as the daughters who remained with the house. As stated, Sarah died, and a few years later, Lucinda did marry. The only brother who would have been in any position to object would have been Lucinda's eldest sibling, Austin, but he was residing in Michigan at the time.

And what of the bones that were found on the site? An article from the *Geneva Times*, published many years earlier, clears up the story.

> *Another village of more ancient date, said to have belonged to the Senecas, was situated on the east side of the creek on the farm now owned by Nathaniel B. Harmon. Some of its ruins were remaining at the arrival*

> *of the first settlers. They had a large field cleared on the bottoms, which gave evidence of having been cultivated for many years, and on which a flourishing apple tree was growing.*
>
> *Their burying place was near the bank, on the spot where Harmon's house now stands. In digging his cellar and grading about the premises, a quantity of human bones were discovered, together with various utensils supposed to have been buried with their owners, among which was a large copper kettle, believed to have been buried in the grave with Bears Oil's mother. The kettle was in a good state of preservation, and is now in Mr. Harmon's family for domestic purposes. Beneath the roots of a large stump, three feet in diameter, which was dug up by Mr. Harmon, was found the entire skeleton of a man above the common size, who had been buried on his face and a root of nearly the thickness of a man's leg growing directly across his neck.*

So, as it turns out, a crime had been committed after all—not the murder of a man named Dan Blakeslee, as had been suggested, but rather the desecration of a Seneca burial site and grave robbing, both of which are deplorable acts to say the least.

28

The Haunted Hut at Portage Lakes

It lacked a door and a window frame, and the chimney of mud and stones had fallen into an unlovely heap, overgrown with rank weeds.
—The Secret of Macarger's Gulch, *by Ambrose Bierce*

It was noted by the *Akron Beacon Journal* in October 1907 that few people still believed in such things as haunted houses. A generation or two earlier, the idea was more commonplace. And yet, at that time, there still stood a few such houses that bore a reputation of having a haunting attached to it. It was brought to the public's attention that one such ancient structure was still standing near the south end of Coventry Township in southern Summit County.

The abandoned hut stood in an old orchard along the north–south road, presently known as State Street, adjoining a tract of land that was owned at that time by Akron businessman Harvey Youngker Hower. The house, it was said, had been built so long ago that little more than rumors existed about its origin. Some believed that it had stood since the earliest days of settlement in the Western Reserve, when much of the land was still inhabited by the Lenape.

The original cabin was constructed of huge timbers of solid oak, eighteen inches square. The upper rafters and floor joists, all that was left of the interior, were made of the same material. Located in one of the upper logs were a few small openings, said to have been used as loopholes, or musket ports, in defense of the place should anyone wish to hinder the occupants. At one point, the cabin had been enlarged by the addition of a frame structure, sided in clapboard and attached to the right side of the small building. This had been done so long ago that it, too, had fallen into a rundown state of abandonment.

It was known that the hut had been occupied for some time by a lone trapper, but whether he was the one who built it, none could say. That man had chosen the spot for his hunting and fishing on account of its proximity to the Portage Lakes, which were more than amply stocked with fish. The dense woodlands along the shores were heavily populated with wild game.

Traditions said that the old trapper was a strange character who seldom spoke to anyone. He occupied that hut in the wilderness until he grew weary of his solitary and lonesome existence. It's said that he took his own life by hanging himself with a rope from one of the huge trees that used to stand near the hut. A number of weeks later, his remains were found hanging from that tree by a passing wayfarer.

Since that time, the hut was said to be haunted. Children dared not to go anywhere near the old building, and even adults, it was said, quaked when they passed by the place on the road after the sun set. Tales were commonly told that at certain times, weird shrieks and howls could be heard coming from the direction of the old house.

A certain elderly man who resided his entire life within the vicinity of the old place and who had died only a few years earlier maintained until his death that he had seen the ghost that inhabited the log house in the orchard. He told how, one time, when he happened to be near that weird place, the thing ran out of the house at him. It was white and had a neck that was fifteen feet long. It chased him eastward to the shores of the West Reservoir, near the State Mill. In terror, he jumped into the reservoir and swam madly for the opposite shore. The thing that was chasing him seemed to be able to swim, too, and jumped into the water after him. It followed him to the middle of the lake, where it stopped and made a strange symbol appear on the surface of the water. The symbol suddenly burst into flames, and just like that, the otherworldly being vanished.

There ends, quite abruptly, the account of the haunted hut at Portage Lakes.

Early records are scarce for Coventry Township, which, until the establishment of Summit County in 1840, was part a of neighboring Portage County. It's difficult to ascertain who, exactly, would have built that cabin, but as traditions maintain, it likely dated to the first days of Ohio. What is known is that the property had fallen into the hands of the Grupe family in the 1830s.

TALE OF A HAUNTED HUT

"Tale of a Haunted Hut." *From the* Akron Beacon Journal, *October 16, 1907.*

Peter Grupe was born in Pennsylvania in 1808. Within a few years, he came with his family to Ohio, where they first settled in Plain Township, Stark County. It was there that he was married to Hannah Kremer in the fall of 1834. Shortly after, the two moved to Coventry Township and took up a living on the farm that contained the old cabin. Hannah passed in 1883, and Peter died the following year. Mr. and Mrs. Grupe were rather well-to-do, but as they had no children of their own, their estate was divided between three friends and a nephew. The small lake on the east end of their property is named for them, but occasionally, it incorrectly appears on some maps as Grape Lake.

In time, the northern section of the former Grupe property fell into the possession of Harvey Hower, who built a sizable cottage near the shores of the West Reservoir called Oakley Villa. As has been the case with many recreational bodies of water, drownings on West Reservoir have sadly been commonplace over the years. Like at Meyers Lake in Canton, there are just too many to count, but one of note occurred in August 1896, when thirty-seven-year-old Cora Lee, a domestic servant for the Hower family, went missing late one night. She was found the next morning by the Howers' eleven-year-old son, Frank, only a few feet from shore. She'd gone to the lake to bathe the previous evening but was believed to have lost consciousness and drowned.

Following the strange account of the haunted hut in 1907, no further mention of it can be found. As it was in a sad state of decline at that time, chances are great that it was deemed by some to be an eyesore and was likely demolished sometime after the article about its bone-chilling history was published. Best estimates of its location put it somewhere in the neighborhood of 4057 State Street, Portage Lakes. As near as can be determined, no trace of it remains today, but then perhaps someone is the wiser and knows more about it.

29
YMCA Camp Centerville Mills

41.347458, -81.334614

And I also firmly believe that Old Norris, our guide, was only half in jest when he told us that story about his night in the haunted house, and that he actually found this camp and dreamed about a letter!
—Balsam Boughs, *by Archibald Campbell Knowles*

Located at the west end of Crackel Road, which runs along the township line between Bainbridge in Geauga County and Aurora in Portage County, was the sleepy community of Centerville Mills. It was established in the very early years of the nineteenth century, just east of present-day Chillicothe Road, or State Route 306, when a sawmill and woolen mill were erected on Smith Creek, which feeds into the Aurora Branch of the Chagrin River.

The mills, which lent their names to that location, were built in 1812 by Colonel John Erastus Jackson of Chester, Massachusetts. He'd arrived earlier that year in the Western Reserve at the age of eighteen with his parents, John and Lovicy, and brother Cyrenius, and he set himself, at once, to the task of clearing a farm and erecting the mills. Within a few years, he was married to Clarissa Tinker of Garrettsville, with whom he raised eight children.

He sold his mills in the 1830s but continued working at his farm. He also became a surveyor and a Baptist minister and preached the gospel. He served two terms as a state senator and died in 1896 following a stroke. He and his family are buried together in the nearby Jackson Family Cemetery on Chillicothe Road.

Within a few years, the mills were purchased by the Cleveland grocery firm of Gorham & Aplin, owned by J.H. Gorham and John Aplin, who kept their store on Superior Street. Attached to the mills was a forty-acre tract of land. The small community of Centerville Mills was a growing concern. It had the milling operation, of course, but nearby sat Paterek Lake, a schoolhouse and a small cluster of homes.

By the 1870s, the mills had been sold to the partnership of Carlton and Bolton, and by 1900, the operation was solely controlled by Mr. Bolton. The site had become popular with picnickers over the years due to its beautiful naturals scenery, most notably its lake, glen, cedar groves, hills and waterfall. All of this beauty attracted the attention of the Young Men's Christian Association (YMCA).

Camp Centerville Mills was officially opened on June 1, 1902, by the YMCA of Greater Cleveland on the forty-acre farm, which was now owned by the Eggleston family. The facility was available to boys under the age of eighteen who were members of the YMCA. Each boy could stay for a week at a time at a cost of $2.50 per week. A large dancing pavilion had recently been built on the site. That was soon to be converted into a dining hall. Also, a number of nearby buildings had been set up as sleeping cabins. These were equipped with spring-frame beds, but the boys had to bring their own bedding. Outdoor tent camping was also available.

Other later amenities included horseshoe pits, tennis and badminton courts, two baseball diamonds, a pool, a boat dock and an archery range. Oh, and just one more thing. There was also a haunted house.

At the start of the 1908 season, it was stated: "Not far away is a house that is said to be haunted, which adds greatly to the interest of the place. The young campers seem to enjoy visiting the desolate structure after nightfall, when they go in numbers."

Most claims date the house to the early 1830s. The identity of the builder remains unknown, but the house was likely built for the milling operation, either by a member of the Jackson family or another later mill owner, possibly to house the family who ran the mills.

Aside from being known as the haunted house, the small, two-story frame residence was also referred to as The White House. It sat directly across Crackel Road from the dining hall. The interior was finished in elegant woodwork, including knotty pine paneling. While it sat empty and unused when the YMCA first established Camp Centerville Mills, in later years, it was utilized as the camp director's residence. The camp permanently closed at the end of the 2004 season, and now, the grounds exist as Centerville

Top: The last known image of the haunted house at Camp Centerville Mills. *Photo courtesy of the* Chagrin Valley Times.

Bottom: Camp Centerville Mills, circa 1922. *Photo courtesy of the Springfield College Archives and Special Collections, the Cliff Smith Postcard Collection.*

An empty, grassy lot now marks the former site of the haunted house at Camp Centerville Mills. *Photo by Lesley Patterson.*

Mills Park, which is owned by Bainbridge Township. Many of the buildings have been torn down, but the dining hall has recently been renovated and is available to rent for special events.

The haunted house across the road, which carried the address 270 Crackel Road, was afterward rented to a family, though it was still owned by Bainbridge Township as part of Centerville Mills Park. Sadly, the house was in dire need of structural repairs and updates, which Bainbridge trustees didn't see as being feasible. They notified the tenants that their lease would be expiring and that the house would be coming down.

In a terrible tragedy, the house caught fire on the night of January 11, 2014. By the time firefighting crews arrived on the scene, the flames were already coming through the roof and more than half of the structure was engulfed in flames. The tenants weren't home at the time, but sadly, they lost their three dogs in the blaze.

Today, the site of the haunted house at Camp Centerville Mills is an empty lot on a slight rise along the south side of Crackel Road, directly across from the old dining hall. One of the most popular attractions in the area, the nearby waterfalls just southwest of where the haunted house was located, are now entirely surrounded by private property and are completely inaccessible to the public.

30
The Ghost of Perry's Flagship

41.554850, -81.609925

The helmsman steered, the ship moved on;
Yet never a breeze unblew;
The mariners all 'gan work the ropes,
Where they were wont to do;
They raised their limbs like lifeless tools—
We were a ghastly crew.
—*"Rime of the Ancient Mariner," by Samuel Taylor Coleridge*

In order to tell this next story, we must first go all the way back to 1813.

For more than a year, the United States was embroiled in a bloody war with Great Britain. In the years that followed the American Revolution, the young nation found difficulty at every turn with its former adversary, primarily out on the ocean. As a nation, the United States wished to trade with other countries, but the British, who were at war with Napoleonic Europe, worried that American goods might make their way into their enemy's hands. Thus, a blockade of the United States was enacted.

Great Britain also needed sailors to aid in the fight against Napoleon. Thus, it turned to American mariners. First, it tried to entice men to join its ranks with a promise of good pay, but if that didn't work, these men would be pressed into the service of the Royal Navy and forced aboard. The final straw was the arming of American Indians in the Northwest Territory. This was the breaking point for the United States. The War of 1812 commenced.

Early in the conflict, the United States lost key battles that might have secured an early end to the war. Unfortunately, these losses resulted in the surrender of important settlements along the northern border with Canada, including Detroit. When Detroit fell to the British, the United States lost its supply line to the rest of the Northwest.

Another early setback in the war was the loss of fighting vessels on the upper lakes, those being the four Great Lakes above Niagara Falls and Lake Ontario. These lakes included, of course, Lake Erie. Dominating those upper lakes, the British now had designs on an invasion of Ohio. In early 1813, the British laid siege to Fort Meigs in present-day Perrysburg, Ohio, and, that summer, attacked Fremont, then called Fort Stevenson.

It was apparent that both sides had come to a stalemate, as far as the upper lakes and the Northwest were concerned. A realization set in. Whoever controlled the lakes would have the upper hand. The British maintained a fleet of five fighting vessels on the lakes, with a sixth being built at Fort Malden in present-day Amherstburg, Ontario. Meanwhile, the United States was assembling a squadron of its own at Erie, Pennsylvania. A few small vessels were already on hand and at the ready, with six more under construction, those being four schooners and two heavier, much larger brigs. The first of these brigs was called the *Niagara*, in honor of a recent U.S. victory on the Niagara River. The second was christened the *Lawrence* in honor of Captain James Lawrence, a gallant naval officer who'd recently been killed in action.

Upon the completion of these vessels, the squadron sailed from Erie to Put-in-Bay, Ohio, where they effectively severed the British supply lines across the lake to Fort Malden.

Control of this new American squadron was placed under the command of a young master commandant named Oliver Hazard Perry of Rhode Island. He'd been sent out to Erie from the East Coast earlier that year to supervise the final stages of the fleet's construction and then affect a blockade of the enemy's base on the Canadian shore. Perry had been a personal friend of the late Captain Lawrence and selected the brig that bore his name to serve as his flagship.

With the American fleet now strategically positioned at Put-in-Bay, supplies were unable to reach the British, and they were left with two options: surrender their fort and retreat back east by land or come out and fight. They opted for the second course of action.

In the early morning hours of September 10, 1813, the masthead lookout of Perry's flagship, the U.S. brig *Lawrence*, sighted the sails of the British squadron some miles distant to the northwest. Perry quickly ordered all nine vessels in the American squadron to weigh anchors and make sail to engage the enemy.

It was slow-going at first, as Perry's fleet fought against an unfavorable wind, but by 10:00 a.m., the wind had shifted, and Perry was able to bring his gunboats into close action. The battle commenced just before noon with the British firing the first shots. By 12:15 p.m., both sides were engaged, if only in part. For reasons that are still debated to this day, Perry's second in command, a man named Jesse Duncan Elliott, who commanded the *Niagara*, shortened sails at the start of the battle and remained over a mile away from the action and well out of range of the enemy cannon fire.

After two and a half hours of fighting, Perry's flagship was a floating wreck. Nearly 80 percent of his crew were either killed or wounded, and he no longer had any working guns on his engaged side. It was around that time that he saw the *Niagara* finally make sail and approach. Perry quickly ordered five men into a longboat and ordered them to row him to the approaching *Niagara*. Dodging a hailstorm of musket and cannon fire, he miraculously reached the *Niagara* unscathed. Taking command of that vessel, he charged at the British and opened fire.

The British had also suffered heavy casualties. Their two largest fighting vessels, HMS *Detroit* and HMS *Queen Charlotte*, were under the command of junior officers, their captains and first officers being killed or critically wounded. Upon seeing this fresh brig joining the action, the British made the decision to wear ship, that is, turn their boats around and bring their previously unused guns to bear. Unfortunately, in doing so, one vessel turned too soon, and the two ships ran afoul of each other, tangling up their rigging. Unable to move, this put a hole in the British battle line. Perry took advantage of the blunder, broke through their line and set up devastating cannon fire across their bows and sterns, raking their decks with deadly precision. One by one, the British struck their colors, and in fifteen minutes, the entire British squadron on Lake Erie surrendered to Perry.

When the fighting had ceased, Perry sent word to the British that he would accept their formal surrender back on the main deck of the *Lawrence*. He had his men row him back over to his flagship, where he penned his famous letter to General William Henry Harrison, which started with the immortal line: "We have met the enemy and they are ours."

The action that day came to be known as the Battle of Lake Erie. It marks the only time in history when an entire British squadron was taken in combat.

The U.S. brig *Lawrence* at the Battle of Lake Erie, September 10, 1813. *Library of Congress.*

The war raged on for another year before peace was finally achieved. Even at that, it was an uneasy peace. There were still instances in which British and American vessels encountered each other and harsh disagreements ensued. It was a worry that another war might erupt if some action wasn't taken. At this, two statesmen, one British and one American, came up with a compromise. Both sides would disarm on the Great Lakes, maintaining a very small and minimally armed force. All other vessels of war were to be dismantled or scuttled. The Rush-Bagot Agreement, signed in 1817, is one of the longest-standing treaties between nations, and it is still in effect to this day.

After the ratification of the agreement, the two U.S. brigs that fought in the Battle of Lake Erie were sunk in the shallow waters of Misery Bay at Presque Isle in Erie, Pennsylvania. In 1876, the *Lawrence* was brought up from the muddy bottom, hauled out of the lake and shipped to Philadelphia, where it was rebuilt and put on display inside a large barn. This was all done in celebration of the centennial of the United States. In an unfortunate turn of events, the barn caught fire and burned to the ground, and along with it, Perry's flagship, the U.S. brig *Lawrence*, was lost.

Flash forward to 1913. The United States was preparing for another centennial celebration, that being the one hundredth anniversary of Perry's victory at the Battle of Lake Erie. To mark the occasion, the brig *Niagara* was brought up from Misery Bay, but instead of being sent off to another city for restoration, the ship was kept in Erie. The plan was to return the one-hundred-year-old vessel to a state of seaworthiness and to mark the occasion by sailing it around the Great Lakes to much pomp and circumstance.

While that work was underway in Erie, a curious event transpired along the shore of Bratenahl, just east of Cleveland, some ninety miles away.

On the morning of June 13, a man named Ignatz Comers, whose name has also appeared in other records at "Ignac Komar," was out early to go fishing. The man was a well-known spring mushroom hunter, but as it was getting late in the year and mushroom season had waned, he decided to try his hand at bringing in some carp. With some bait, a carp net and a ceramic jug, he made his way down to the stone breakwater behind the old country club that once sat along the lake at the end of Eddy Road, just north of Lake Shore Boulevard. Arriving at the end of the breakwater, Ignatz set his carp trap and sat down on a nearby rock to await developments. It was an unusually chilly morning for mid-June, and an impenetrable mist was lying on the water.

The country club at the north end of Eddy Road in Bratenahl, circa 1892. *Photo courtesy the Western Reserve Historical Society.*

Ignatz yawned and shivered. Whether it was after the yawn or before the shiver, the man could not recall, but suddenly, he was startled by the muffled tolling of a bell and the clanking and rattling of chains issuing from the fog. Then, before his eyes, loomed the hull of a boat. But such a boat Ignatz had never seen before. To him, the vessel seemed ridiculous, with its tall masts and more yardarms and rigging than anything he'd ever laid his eyes on. There also appeared to be a line of portholes along the side, from which pointed the black muzzles of what Ignatz took to be cannons.

Although he could see men moving about, not one human voice ushered forth. The eerie crew swarmed about the deck and clambered through the rigging, obeying unheard commands. What's more, they were what Ignatz Comers described as "funny looking, whiskered, bare of leg, and with trousers rolled up to their knees."

The man claimed that he would have hailed the passing vessel if he could have, but his lips refused to open. All he could do was stare. And while he stared, the clanking and rattling stopped and the tolling died away, but the ghost ship sailed in the fog and the crew still swarmed the deck.

A present-day view of the breakwater at the former country club in Bratenahl, where the ghost of the brig *Lawrence* was believed to have been sighted. *Photo by William G. Krejci.*

A moment later, the watchman for the clubhouse called over to him, abruptly breaking his gaze from the vessel. The watchman believed that Ignatz Comers had been sleeping on the breakwater, to which Ignatz disagreed, but still, the watchman prodded him with his club to move along. At this, he gathered up his trap and strolled away, but looking into the mist, he wondered where the phantom vessel had gone.

He later found his friend Vladimir Morris, who worked the grounds at Gordon Park, and Farrall English, who worked at town hall. He shared his experience with his friends, who, in turn, shared the experience with others. Upon the insistence that Ignatz Comers was not asleep, the encounter was duly authenticated by Bratenahl's most prominent raconteurs. It was their general opinion that he had actually witnessed the passing ghost of Oliver Hazard Perry's long-lost flagship, the U.S. brig *Lawrence*. Some suggested that the vessel was jealous of all the attention the *Niagara* was getting and wanted to make a show of itself.

Some might think that this was actually the *Niagara* undergoing sea trials, but the *Niagara* was still in Erie being rigged when Ignatz Comers experienced the ghostly visitation.

31

The Underground Railroad Stop

41.024143, -80.640050

But the music, the supernatural, weird, and ghostly music, went on, and then—ah! then—the final manifestation appeared.
—The Humbling of the Memblings, *by Walter Besant*

In Joseph G. Butler's book *History of Youngstown and the Mahoning Valley*, published in 1921, we find a story that speaks on the little community of Cook's Corners, named for the Philo Cook family who resided in that section of Boardman Township, Mahoning County. This following account was brought to my attention by Gavin Esposito. The first part reads:

> *Reference has been made elsewhere in this work to the fact that the Quakers are on records as the first group of people in this country to formally protest against human slavery. To Quakers also belongs the honor of conducting the first if not the only station on the celebrated "Underground Railway," by which route many slaves fleeing from bondage were assisted to reach Canada and freedom. These two Quakers were William and Mary Henry, and they lived during the '60s in a humble home on the south side of the Boardman Road, about 1,500 feet west of Cook's Corners. Here they had arranged an inside room with the door concealed from observation, and in this room they kept such slaves as made their way past the place northward until they could be assisted to the next "station" on the "Underground Railway."*

It's true that the Quakers, or Society of Friends, led the way in the abolitionist movement and were very active as conductors on the Underground Railroad. It's also a very good probability that the house mentioned here was used for the purpose stated. There are, however, a couple of small inaccuracies within the account.

Delving into the historical research aspect, census records, maps and tax records tell us that the names of the couple who operated this stop in assisting freedom seekers to the North were John and Nancy Henry, not William and Mary, as suggested.

John Henry, a weaver by trade, was born in Ireland around 1803. He arrived in the area around 1820 and first settled in neighboring Poland Township, where he was married on May 30, 1822, to Nancy Reed, who originally hailed from Virginia. Their marriage was officiated by Reverend James Wright, a Presbyterian minister. In 1825, they relocated to Boardman, about a mile west, where they took up residency on a sixteen-acre-tract of land located between the Cook and Bishop family farms. There they remained until Nancy's death, which occurred on March 2, 1855. She was laid to rest in the Poland Presbyterian Cemetery on North Hine Circle.

On March 11 the following year, John was married to Susanna Howard in Mahoning County. Within a couple of years, they were living in Deerfield Township, Portage County. By 1880, John Henry had died, and Susanna was living in Ellsworth, Mahoning County, with her brother.

By 1860, the farmhouse that previously belonged to John and Nancy Henry was owned and occupied by Hiram Gano Gulick; his wife, Mary Spence-Gulick; and their daughters, Isabella and Mary. The Gulick family had come to Ohio from New York, and Hiram had taken on the role of a farmer. By 1870, he, his wife and their youngest child had moved back east and taken up residency in New Jersey. Isabelle Gulick remained in Ohio and became a schoolteacher in Niles, where she taught future President William McKinley. By all indications, the Gulicks were members of the Methodist Episcopal Church. This is shown in Isabelle's death notice many years later and in the fact that her brother, Charles, attended Wesleyan University, which was established by the Methodist Episcopal Church.

The point here is that neither the Henrys or the Gulicks, who occupied the house that was an alleged Underground Railroad stop, were members of the Society of Friends, or Quakers. This doesn't disqualify any of them from possibly assisting in that noble cause, nor does it exclude their former home from carrying the reputation of having been haunted. The rest of the story from Butler's book on Youngstown and the Mahoning Valley continued with this claim:

> *For many years after these gentle but courageous people passed away, their little house was unoccupied, and gradually there grew up a belief that it was haunted. This belief arose from stories told by neighbors of seeing spectral groups of colored people and hearing the sound of banjos. Doubtless the stories were imaginary enlargements of occasional glimpses the unsuspecting neighbors had of runaway slaves during the period when its occupants were lending their aid to the cause of freedom in spite of the fact that to do so they had to violate the written law. But whatever suspicion may attach to the ghost stories, there is no doubt as to the runaway slaves who found refuge with this quiet Quaker couple until they could be transported under cover of darkness to the next point of safety, which was fifteen miles away in Trumbull County.*

It's unknown when, exactly, the house was demolished. Today, the site of the former stop on the Underground Railroad, which later carried a ghostly reputation, is somewhere in the front parking lot of Presidential Square shopping center between South Avenue and Eisenhower Drive.

32

A Haunting on Hemlock Road

41.378391, -81.626494

All is silent and drear! The long years fled away,
And its tenants are loneliness, mould and decay;
The lone villager passing at nightfall the dell,
Holds some talisman the closer, or mutters a spell;
The windows are broken and tapestries flap,
As a nest for the moth, or a lurk for the bat;
Rank weeds fill the pathway, or flaunt o'er the eaves,
Where the spider his web all in solitude weaves.
—*"The Haunted House," by Edward Sprague Rand Jr.*

In 1868, a small brick manufacturing company began operating in Independence Township, along the west bank of the Cuyahoga River, where Hemlock and Stone Roads met at the bottom of the hill. In time, plans for a railroad to service the area were presented, and by 1880, the Valley Railway was opened, connecting Cleveland to Canton. With the opening of the railroad, so, too, came a number of little whistle-stops along the way, small communities that sprang up around the train stations, which, in some cases, were a mile or two from their respective towns. Thus a small cluster of buildings that became a community known as Independence Station was established near the brick works.

Not long after, a village was laid out, and lots were subdivided. It was a small community with only four streets, those being Riverside, Clewell, Walnut and Oliver Streets.

In the early 1890s, Independence Station adopted the name South Park. Meanwhile, the brick manufacturing company grew and soon became the Cleveland Hydraulic Press Brick Company. By the early twentieth century, the facility was producing Haydite, a lightweight aggregate used in concrete. South Park doubled as a company town, with more employee housing located slightly up the hill on Hemlock Road.

For many years now, a story has been told about Hemlock Road being haunted by the spirit of an American Indian girl who was sexually assaulted and killed by two settlers in the early 1800s. The narrative goes on to claim that her father, the chief, placed a hex upon the land, and from that day on, the area bore a curse.

This is not that story.

On the morning of Monday, April 4, 1921, news broke of a skeleton that was found in a shallow grave in the basement of a house on Hemlock Road near the small village of South Park. The bones described were found the previous evening, when the premises was being inspected by a man named Sufphare Whitmer, who worked at the nearby brick works and was looking to rent the house.

While Mr. Whitmer was making an examination of the premises, he entered the low basement and noticed that the stone floor had been chiseled through. It was obvious that the grave had been opened within the last couple of days. Whitmer noticed what appeared to be a bone protruding from the recently dug-up soil. He started to dig around it and soon uncovered a bony human arm. He immediately notified police, who continued the excavation, revealing a nearly complete human skeleton that was lying face down. It was noticed, however, that a few bones were missing. These were found to have been recently removed and were later located under a pile of dirt in the corner of the basement, along with a shoe, a black shirt and a pair of corduroy trousers. The bones showed no signs of injury, making it difficult to determine a cause of death.

According to the report, the bones were found to have been buried in the pit and covered with quicklime, or calcium oxide, a caustic substance that was believed to have been used to dissolve the body's soft tissue and destroy any evidence that might identify who the murderer, or murderers, might have been. The grave was just large enough to admit a human body and was eighteen inches deep.

The house where this grim discovery was made was the last of five residences heading up Hemlock Road away from the Hydraulic Press Brick Company. It was positioned directly on the north side of the road, while the

The haunted house on Hemlock Road. *From the* Cleveland Press, *August 25, 1921.*

other four were set a good distance back. It was a red frame house, stood two stories high; it had three rooms and a lean-to on the first floor, with two bedrooms upstairs. Its entrance was located on the right side of the house, and with the exception of two windows, an almost completely blank wall faced the road.

The bones were soon identified as those of a man known commonly to his friends as Black Patsy, who had disappeared more than two years earlier. The *Cleveland Press* reported his proper name as "Pasquale Mago," while the *Plain Dealer* gave his name as "Pasquale Marzo." No information can be found regarding either of those names. Black Patsy was employed in the nearby brickyard and went missing in 1918. It was believed he had gone to work in Detroit.

Curiously, a number of families occupied the house during the time the bones were buried in the basement. Two of those families had abruptly moved out shortly after moving in. One of those former occupants, a Mrs. J.W. Smith, shared with her neighbor Mary Wagner that she had a queer feeling in the house and that it always seemed to have a spooky feeling to it.

Mrs. Smith and her family had moved out on April 1, just two days before the gruesome discovery was made. That evening, a few hours after they left, a light was seen shining from inside the house. It was believed the Smiths were the source of the light, but it was soon learned that they had departed for Pennsylvania earlier that day.

By Monday afternoon, just hours after the story broke, police had a suspect in custody.

As inquiries were made, it was learned that the victim, at the time of his disappearance, had been renting a room in the home for three months from another man, who occupied the murder house with his wife. A short time after the arrest, detectives conducted a search of the suspect's current residence and discovered an arsenal of firearms and ammunition and a sack of lime in the basement, noticing that some had been spilled onto the floor for no apparent reason. Both the suspect and his wife were questioned extensively over the course of the next few days. It had been reported that the wife had suffered from fits of melancholia since their tenant had gone missing two years earlier. Police believed that this might have accounted for the fact that she may have known something about the man's disappearance. It was also noted that the couple moved out of that house and into their current place of residence just days after the disappearance.

Another item found in the suspect's house was a sheet of metal that matched those the neighbors recalled being placed over the windows to act as blinds at the time the couple lived in the house on Hemlock Road. Small holes had been cut into these blinds to act as peepholes, or possibly gun ports. It was also remembered that the upper windows were covered with bars. Neighbors recalled late-night meetings in the house during the time that the suspect and his wife occupied the place. Many started to wonder if the victim, whose bones had been found in the cellar, had been involved in whatever activities were transpiring in the house at those late hours.

William Carmichael, a night watchman at the nearby brick factory, recalled a wagon that used to make trips up to the house around midnight. He got curious one night and decided to follow it. As he approached the house, two shots were fired at him, and he made haste back down the road, deciding not to attempt to follow the wagon again and to forget about his curiosity.

One day during the week before the bones were found, it was said that two men pulled up in front of the house on a red motorcycle. They got off and menacingly approached the door. At the time, the only person who was home was a man named John Washburn, who boarded with the Smith family. He told authorities that he was so alarmed by these two men that he had to warn them off with a pistol. They ultimately got back on the motorcycle and left. None of the neighbors recognized either of the men.

After five days of questioning by police, the suspect and his wife were released, as no solid evidence linking them to a crime could be established. The lime found in their basement was circumstantial evidence at best. Also, the coroner was unable to determine an exact cause of death. The names of the suspect and his wife were withheld from the papers and remain a secret to this day. All that is known is that the man, like most everyone else in this narrative, was an employee of the brick company at the bottom of Hemlock Road.

By that summer, word had begun to circulate that the house on Hemlock Road was haunted. Some claimed that a ghostly wagon, pulled by phantom horses, would lumber up the road at midnight, making its way to the old house from the Cuyahoga Valley below. It was believed that this was the wagon that conveyed the dead man to that house for his burial in the cellar.

That August, a reporter for the *Cleveland Press* decided to spend the night in the haunted house on Hemlock Road. He was awakened numerous times throughout the night. The first time, he woke to what sounded like someone walking on the roof, but this proved to be a tree branch rubbing against the house. He next heard what he believed was someone walking about outside. This turned out to be a neighborhood dog that had wandered into the yard. There was next a loud bang on the roof, which he believed was caused by a falling apple. Aside from the rattling of the windows and the door, which was caused by the wind, he was also awakened several times by crickets, bullfrogs and a mouse. The last disturbance was the sound of a heavy chain being dragged about. For this, he could find no explanation. Still, the reporter maintained his disbelief in otherworldly spirits.

The murder of the man whose skeletal remains were found in a shallow grave in the basement of a house on Hemlock Road was never solved. No suspect was ever charged or convicted. The victim's final place of rest is not known, nor can his birth name be confirmed. The haunted house has long since been torn down, and that section of Hemlock Road is no longer accessible to traffic.

Today, the site lies within the boundaries of Cuyahoga Valley National Park and is located near mile marker 1.3 on the Hemlock Creek Trail, which follows the course of the old road. At the time of this writing, only one of the four houses that were located east of the haunted house is still standing.

Today, the former site of the haunted house on Hemlock Road sits just inside a slightly wooded patch, immediately to the east of the clearing. *Photo by William G. Krejci.*

Please be aware that this house is not the haunted house. "No Trespassing" signs are clearly posted, and the place is monitored by security cameras.

The exact location of the haunted house is immediately to the east of a clearing, where high-tension power lines cross old Hemlock Road. It's a weed-choked, slightly wooded area lying among the brambles and briers. No trace of the haunted house remains.

33

Sunnyside

41.097482, -81.5138776

Looking back at the grotesque peaks and shadowy angles of the old mansion, they fancied a gloom diffused about it, which no brightness of the sunshine could dispel.
—The House of the Seven Gables, *by Nathaniel Hawthorne*

In early March 1922, it was reported that the last haunted house known to the residents of Akron was an old mansion situated on North Hill near the Valley View Club. The house's days were numbered, as workmen were getting ready to tear down the structure in the next few days to make way for the North Hill Viaduct Park.

It was said that, up until a year ago, the house had been occupied by tenants, but for only a few days at a time. They would move out after their short stay, declaring the place to be haunted. These short-term occupants claimed that their articles either moved about on their own or disappeared completely in a most mysterious manner. It was also stated that a rope with a noose tied into it would suddenly appear hanging from the ceiling in one of the rooms.

The name given to this house was "Sunnyside," an ironic name for a house that would later carry such a dark reputation. What's more is that research reveals the property was directly responsible for at least one death.

The story begins with the arrival of Oliver Nox Mosser of Allentown, Pennsylvania. Mosser was born there in 1848 and ultimately became a physician. He visited Ohio on occasion, and it was on one such visit that he

Sunnyside, which sat at 47 Olive Street, on the brow of North Hill. *Photo courtesy of the Akron-Summit County Public Library.*

met Catherine "Cathrina" Stauffer of Clinton, Ohio. The two were married in 1874 and raised three children. In February 1876, the Mossers moved to Akron and purchased five acres of the Burrows Tract on the south side of Olive Street, just east of North Howard Street, on Akron's North Hill. Another 2.65 acres would later be added. Mosser purchased the lot with the intention of building a fine residence on the site. Construction on that beautiful home commenced that summer.

The home, which he'd named Sunnyside, was built at 47 Olive Street on the southern brow of North Hill. It had a commanding view of Akron, just to the south, across the valley where the Little Cuyahoga flowed. The house was constructed of brick and stood three stories high. It featured all modern amenities. Every room was heated, and hot and cold running water serviced each floor. The interior was exquisitely finished in the finest materials available. At the center of the first floor was the large double hall, which opened to all the other rooms on that floor. The grand dining room measured fifteen feet by twenty-four feet and could accommodate a large number of guests. There were parlors and sitting rooms, a large kitchen, a butler's pantry and storage rooms. Four bedrooms were located on the second floor, two of which were larger than the dining room. Two more bedrooms were located on the third floor, likely occupied by the serving staff. The basement had a large pump that forced water from the well to a holding tank on the top floor.

A large wooden barn was also erected on the property, just to the east of the house. The Mossers planted numerous fruit-bearing trees, including peach, pear, apple, plum, quince and apricot trees. There were also many grape vineyards and berry bushes placed about the yard. Such a residence as this would seem like a paradise, but even the most beautiful of settings can turn tragic.

On the evening of Friday, February 2, 1883, a girl named Mary Strapp celebrated her fifteenth birthday with her family at their home on nearby Tallmadge Avenue. The following morning, she walked to the house of John Kennedy and his family, who lived down the hill along North Howard Street, just south of Glenwood Avenue. The home was set close to a shallow ravine that descended the hill from near the Mosser property, about 1,500 feet to the north. The rain was coming down heavily that morning, but Mary made haste to the Kennedys' home nonetheless. She'd been hired to help Mrs. Kennedy pack, as they were moving to a new house in Mount Vernon. The day went on rather uneventfully, and the rain continued to fall.

It should be noted here that the little ravine that ran down the hill alongside North Howard Avenue was the drainage route for an area of close to three thousand acres. Around 1877, a roadway was built behind Sunnyside, leading from North Howard Street up to the back of the property. It was stated that Oliver Mosser had built this, while Mosser claimed that it had been built at the order of F.A. Burrows, who owned the adjoining property. In any case, whoever the builder was, they needed to cross the little ravine that ran from the back of the property along North Howard. Thus, they filled in the creek and built up an elevated roadway, constructed of sand and earth, across the stream. To allow water to continue to flow its course, they placed a small pipe at the base of this new roadway. Unfortunately, the pipe was far too small to sufficiently drain the amount of water that was flowing through the gully. Thus, the constructed roadway acted as a dam. Throughout the day, the water continued to accumulate, forming a lake behind it with a depth of over ten feet, backing up over a half a mile upstream.

At around 2:30 p.m., the earthen dam gave way, and all hell broke loose.

The first house in the flood's path was that of Harrison Geer and his family. The water hit with such force that it knocked the house off its foundation and carried Mrs. Geer and her three children out the door. They were swept across Glenwood Avenue and were caught on the fence of a property owned by the Grimwood family, who came out of their house and aided in their rescue.

As the water raced farther down the run, fences, trees and other debris were picked up and carried along, smashing everything in their path as they went.

While all of this was unfolding, Mary Strapp was standing in the Kennedys' yard, dumping out a pan of water when she heard a rumbling sound coming from up the little ravine. At this, she came running back into the kitchen, slamming the door behind her and calling out for Mrs. Kennedy. Suddenly, the kitchen door burst inward, and a massive torrent of water ripped through the house. Mrs. Kennedy hurried her children up the stairs as quickly as she could, but as she turned for Mary Strapp, she found the girl had already been washed out of the house and was holding onto a pear tree just outside the kitchen window. Before Mrs. Kennedy could reach her, she was dragged from the tree by the current and was carried off by the flood, the waters of which were now running between four and six feet deep. Mrs. Kennedy watched with heart-wrenching helplessness as the girl was carried away to her death.

A few days later, Mary Strapp's remains were found lying face up among a cluster of trees on the property of George Cartwright along the west bank of the Little Cuyahoga between locks 19 and 20. The force of the water had carried her almost a mile and a half downstream. That spring, multiple lawsuits were filed against the Mossers regarding the flood. Among those who filed were Mary Strapp's father, John, who sought damages in the amount of $4,000. All cases were dismissed.

Around 1885, Oliver Mosser started looking at possibly selling his home on the brow of North Hill. That December, the home was suggested as a good possible site for the town's children's home, which was seeking a new location. The idea was passed on, but the home was looked at again for that use in 1889. Unfortunately, the property had already been sold to another.

On January 9, 1889, it was announced that Oliver N. Mosser had sold his beautiful home on North Hill and would shortly be moving with his family to Tennessee, where he'd recently bought a large tract of land. Oliver Mosser followed up on that plan, moved to Tennessee and took up farming. He died in Viola, Tennessee, on March 27, 1930, at the age of eighty-one.

As it turns out, Oliver Mosser had sold Sunnyside to the Kubler family.

Edward George Kubler—or George, as he preferred—was born in Munich, Germany, on February 26, 1846, and immigrated in August 1869 to the United States, where he first entered business in New York City. In 1873, he was married to Emilie Sophie Duchard of Hennepin, Illinois. Together, they raised five children. In February 1878, the Kublers came to Akron,

Edward George Kubler. *From* Illustrated Summit County, Ohio, *1891.*

where George founded the Akron Varnish Company, which kept its office at Main and State Streets.

For the last few years, the Kubler family had been residing at 110 Park Place. Lately, George had been living in Germany, where he'd been working at expanding the company's interests. That September, after an announcement was made regarding the Kublers' purchase of Sunnyside, Mrs. Kubler took their children on a trip to Germany to visit their father. The entire family returned in November 1889 and took up residency in their new house on North Hill.

For the next few years, the Kublers lived on and off between Germany and Akron. Finally, on March 3, 1897, George Kubler offered his house and barn for sale or for rent. Though he placed an enticing advertisement in the papers, describing the grounds as being covered with all kinds of the choicest fruit trees and berries, there were no takers.

In 1906, George Kubler moved to Brussels for work. He returned to the United States briefly in 1907, but the following year, he was back in Europe. He died on March 19, 1909, in Freiburg, Germany, and was buried in Frankfurt. Emilie Kubler continued to own the house and property on North Hill but didn't live there. By 1910, she was residing in a home at 111 East Market Street. She decided to rent out the house, but for reasons stated in the opening of this chapter, occupants didn't remain there long.

In January 1921, a new viaduct project was started. The high-level bridge would connect downtown Akron with the North Hill neighborhood. It was realized almost at once that that the construction of this bridge would compromise the Kubler property, among others. The house was demolished the following spring, and the viaduct opened that October with a span of 2,800 feet and a height of 130 feet.

On June 2, 1923, it was announced that the Kubler lot had been selected as the site for the new Catholic hospital. The deal was closed by Mrs. Kubler's attorney, as she had since moved to Germany. The following year, St. Thomas Hospital was built on the site, which also covered the grounds of the former Valley View Club immediately to the west.

A present-day view of the former site of Sunnyside on Olive Street in Akron. *Photo by William G. Krejci.*

Emilie Kubler died in Germany in 1925 and was laid to rest beside her husband in Frankfurt.

The viaduct, which precipitated the demolition of Sunnyside, closed in 1977 and was torn down the following year. It was replaced by the current Y-Bridge. St. Thomas Hospital was demolished in 2024. At the time of this writing, the former location of Sunnyside is a construction site. What's to occupy the site in the future, the readers will have to discover for themselves.

34
The Hotchkiss Mansion Haunting

41.160871, -81.257821

All day within the dreamy house,
The doors upon their hinges creak'd;
The blue fly sung in the pane; the mouse
Behind the mouldering wainscot shriek'd,
Or from the crevice peer'd about.
Old faces glimmer'd thro' the doors
Old footsteps trod the upper floors,
Old voices called her from without.
She only said, "My life is dreary,
He cometh not," she said;
She said, "I am aweary, aweary,
I would that I were dead!"
—"Mariana," *by Alfred, Lord Tennyson*

We turn our attention from one beautiful mansion to another. This home was located on Oakwood Street in the city of Ravenna, Portage County. Construction of this fine residence started in early 1867 and was completed that November. The main part of the house, constructed of sandstone taken from a quarry on the property, stood two stories high and was capped by a beautiful central cupola. It featured many large rooms that were trimmed extravagantly in woodwork, tall windows and multiple fireplaces. It was located on a tract of 27.62

acres that had been laid out as a garden-like setting, complete with tall pines and a serene reflective pond. The cost of building this residence was $10,000, an incredible sum at that time, especially when a house that cost half that amount was considered a mansion. Its builder was Mr. Harvey Hotchkiss, an early pioneer of that town.

Born in Plymouth, Litchfield County, Connecticut, on June 5, 1804, Harvey Hotchkiss came to Ohio in March 1824 with his parents, Lyman and Lois Sperry Hotchkiss, making the entire journey by land. Originally, he resided on his father's farm, which contained many acres northwest of town. On June 6, 1825, he was wed to Ann Jenette Bradshaw. The following year, they moved onto a farm about a mile and a half north of town. He and Ann became the parents of two children, Flora, who died at the age of five, and George, who survived to adulthood. Ann passed away on June 18, 1850. On November 19, 1853, Hotchkiss was married again, this time to Sylvia Adeline Webster, a recent widow of one Mr. Ross. Shortly after, he sold his farm and moved to a house that stood on the northeast corner of present-day North Chestnut Street and Washington Avenue. In 1867, Harvey Hotchkiss purchased the large tract on Oakwood Street and built his fine mansion.

For many years, the Hotchkiss mansion stood as a silent sentinel, watching as the city of Ravenna grew around it, and by 1924, it had earned a reputation of being haunted. That August, an article appeared in the *Akron Beacon Journal* that told a wild tale of the original owner of the Hotchkiss mansion.

The article spoke of the fiery spirit of an old sea captain that aimlessly roamed the house, lurking behind the locked doors and heavily shuttered windows of the Hotchkiss homestead on Oakwood Street, silently awaiting the return of his shipmates. It was explained that a century or more earlier, an old and bearded captain of the sea, with hair as white as the caps of the waves in the haven from whence he came, tired of the roll and toss of the billowing sea, of the tangy salted atmosphere, and sought some inward shelter to soothe him in his declining years.

The massive house stood on the hill with its quaint, picturesque beauty, the tall and stately pine trees that surrounded it, the winding walkway to the street and the little pond to the left of it, suggesting only sheer beauty to please the vanity of the retired sailor.

Many years earlier, the article explained, Ravenna held no more beautiful spot than that castle on the hill and its twenty-six acres of magnificence. Now, the estate's pleasing appearance had transformed into rustic quaintness.

A view of the Hotchkiss house. *From the* Panoramic View of the City of Ravenna, Portage Co., Ohio, *1882*.

The once winding walkway of boards had now become the habitat of spiders, wasps and all other form of crawling creatures. The little pond was overgrown with a thick layer of weeds, waterlilies and rushes. The mansion, slowly deteriorating, was now netted in ivy that had grown around it, where the fragrance of roses once pervaded and sprightly flowers pushed their faces toward the sunlight.

Many people about the community were now saying that the original owner of the mansion, who was unknown to most but was now suggested as being the former sea captain previously mentioned, had died a most mysterious death while taking his daily bath. They further alleged that his ghost could now be seen walking from the nearby quarry to his house, seeking revenge against his unknown murderer.

The quarry spoken of was the same one that the stone used to build the house was taken from. It also supplied stone for the foundations of other early houses of Ravenna, as well as a stone barn that once sat close to the Hotchkiss property but was now owned by a man named Michael Eichler. Since it was abandoned many years earlier, the quarry was now filled with water to a depth of twenty feet.

A good number of the elderly residents of Ravenna shot down the story of the ghostly sea captain and his mysterious murder, saying that neither their fathers, nor their father's fathers, had ever told such tales, and they said these stories were the concoctions of the younger generation. Still, Ravenna Police Chief John C. Goodenough insisted that the place was haunted and warned the romantic-minded youth of Ravenna to keep well away from its inky shadows. Kate Hotchkiss, the granddaughter of Harvey Hotchkiss and the owner of the house at the time this article was written, didn't express an opinion one way or the other on whether the house was haunted.

Still, it was said that the old mansion's uninhabited atmosphere—its leering, grotesque exterior; its sounds of owls at night; and its old and stately pines that glimpsed over the top of scrub trees—held the passerby enthralled with wonder and marvel.

It should be pointed out, as stated at the start of this chapter, that Harvey Hotchkiss was, in fact, the builder of the Hotchkiss mansion. What's more, in all his days, he never sailed the high seas. He was a farmer his entire life, nothing more and nothing less. To put one last point on the matter, there was no mystery surrounding the death of Harvey Hotchkiss, which occurred on November 17, 1871.

On the evening of Thursday, November 16, Mr. Hotchkiss had been feeling as well as he had at any time during the last several months. He stayed up with his wife and family, conversing with them until around ten o'clock that night, at which time he retired to bed. He was asleep soon after, and his wife, Sylvia, who was awake for another hour, noted that he seemed to be sleeping soundly and breathing freely.

At about four o'clock in the morning, Mrs. Hotchkiss awoke and found her husband lying in his usual position on his left side. She discovered that his feet were cold, and laying her hand on his forehead, she found that it, too, was cold. She then took hold of his shoulders and shook him, calling aloud to him, but there was no response. Becoming alarmed, she hastily arose, sent for a physician and called in her near neighbors, but it was all to no avail. His spirit had departed this world. Without struggle or even moving a muscle, he passed to his eternal rest.

For more than twenty years, he had been subject to epileptic seizures, which had greatly affected his general health. Having been quite ill the previous spring, he made his own funeral arrangements, including which minister would officiate the service and who his pallbearers would be. It was written into his last will and testament at that time, and this was put into use two days after his passing. Harvey Hotchkiss was sixty-two at the time of his death. He was interred at Maple Grove Cemetery in Ravenna.

In time, the house passed into the hands of Harvey Hotchkiss's only surviving child, George. Following the death of George Hotchkiss in 1906, the property came into the hands of his youngest child, Kate.

In 1947, Kate Hotchkiss sold the family estate, which, at the time, comprised the grand mansion and twenty-six acres of land, to the City of Ravenna. The land was to be converted into the new Ravenna City Park. A major kerfuffle, however, arose over what to do with the Hotchkiss mansion. The house was in pretty bad shape at that point, having not been occupied for many years. Every single window on the house was broken. The doors had been torn from their hinges. Plaster had been kicked off the walls, and the plumbing had been destroyed. City councilmen believed that the house was in good enough condition to be saved, with restoration costs sitting between $3,000 and $5,000. It was their plan to convert the old house into a park shelter. Mayor Thomas Ritenour and his park commissioner, Cyril Fulweber, wanted the home to be demolished. Ritenour said that he'd make every effort to have the house torn down.

The Hotchkiss mansion was located directly in front of this water tower at Ravenna City Park. *Photo by Lesley Patterson.*

On Saturday, June 4, 1949, the issue came to an unexpected and unfortunate resolution. Neighbors made frantic calls at noon to report that someone had set the Hotchkiss mansion on fire. Interestingly enough, it was realized that the fire department was already on site and had been for quite some time before the fire broke out. By all appearances, the mayor and park commissioner had ordered the fire to be set without the approval of city council or the park board and against the wishes of many in the community who wanted to see the home saved. The mayor and park commissioner both maintained that the fire had been ignited from an "undetermined origin." The next day, what remained of the Hotchkiss mansion was bulldozed. In the days that immediately followed, all three members of the park board resigned in protest. Commissioner Fulweber resigned two weeks later over the flack he received for ordering the house to be torched.

Today, the site of the Hotchkiss mansion is occupied by Ravenna City Park. The location of the house was about 150 feet northeast of the water tower. No trace remains.

35

THE ATTIC GHOST AT REX'S TAVERN

40.979933, -81.534126

Old in name The Haunted Tavern holds the barren rise alone—
Standing high in air deserted, ghost-like long itself has grown.
—*"King's Tavern," by John James Piatt*

If you happen to find yourself out and about exploring some of the locations featured in this book, you may be surprised to learn that more than a couple of them are, by mere coincidence, located rather close to each other. Such is the case of our next destination. If you happen to be near the general location of the haunted hut at Portage Lakes and are looking to take a break from your travels, you're in luck. Refreshments are close at hand. Simply head south on State Street and turn left onto West Turkeyfoot Lake Road, or State Route 619, as it's also designated. Continue east for not even half a mile, cross over the Turkeyfoot Lake Channel and pull into the parking lot on your left at 357 West Turkeyfoot Lake Road, New Franklin. Go inside, pull up a stool and order your favorite beverage.

Congratulations, you're now drinking in the Upper Deck, one of the oldest original buildings in Summit County, second only to the David Hudson House in Hudson, which dates to 1806. Two older buildings exist at Hale Farm & Village in Bath but were brought there from neighboring counties. You also happen to be sitting in a place that carries a legend of a haunting that has been forgotten for far too long.

This story begins with a man named George Adam Rex, who was born about 1778 in Northampton County, Pennsylvania. Around 1804, he married Anna Maria "Polly" Spengler, with whom he had six children. Three years later, he and his new family arrived in Northeast Ohio and first put down roots in Plain Township, just north of Canton. It was there where George Rex built his first gristmill in 1811 on Nimishillen Creek. Seeing its success, he soon added a sawmill. A few years later, he sold the site to a man named John Shorb and relocated to Franklin Township, about thirteen miles northwest. This was still a part of Stark County at the time, as Summit County wasn't established until 1840.

There, in 1816, Rex purchased a small tract of land and set himself to the task of building a dam at the narrow outlet of Turkeyfoot Lake. He soon put up a gristmill on the site. This was followed immediately after by the construction of a large, L-shaped, three-story brick home. The bricks used in the construction were made on a neighboring farm that belonged to a man named Abraham Schwartz. The flooring was made of oak. Hand-forged spikes secured the heavy beams, and the stairs were held in place with great wooden pegs. The house was built to double as a tavern stand, which serviced that section of the stagecoach route that ran from Pittsburgh to Sandusky and points west. George Rex later added a distillery, sawmill and fulling mill for processing wool to the operation.

A historic image of the The Old Homestead Inn, originally Rex's Taven, later the White House Tavern and presently the Upper Deck, circa 1930. *Photo courtesy of the Thornton family and the Portage Lakes Photograph Collection, the Portage Lakes Historical Society and the Akron-Summit County Public Library.*

Sadly, Polly Rex died just two years later on March 6, 1818. Four months after her passing, George Rex married Christiana Weaver and, with her, fathered four additional children. Over the next decade and a half, George Rex accumulated additional lands, amounting to well over six hundred acres.

It had been said in later years that Rex ran out of money in the 1830s and was forced to sell his property, but this wasn't the case at all. George Adam Rex died in January 1834 at the age of fifty-six. His second wife, Christiana, died quite suddenly the following year.

In 1836, the estate of George and Christiana Rex, including the former Rex's Tavern on Turkeyfoot Lake, was listed for sale. The notice read:

> *"Valuable Property for Sale"*
>
> *The Undersigned wish to sell the Farm and Mill property formerly owned by G.A. Rex, situated in the north part of Stark County, adjoining Portage, and a short distance east of the Ohio Canal.*
>
> *There are 665 Acres of Land, about 180 of which are under cultivation. A large and commodious Brick House, designed for a dwelling house, Tavern and Store, a large and excellent Barn, and a Grist Mill are upon the premises. The Water Power is believed to be sufficient for three pair of mill stones and perhaps more. The whole can be purchased lower than any property of equal value in this vicinity. The title is indisputable. Those desirous of making a good bargain are invited to call. Further information may be obtained from Silliman, Stetson & Barr. No. 5 Franklin Buildings, Cleveland.*

The entirety of the property was sold to John and Catharine Swartz Thornton from Snyder County, Pennsylvania, who used the large brick tavern as a residence. Henceforth, the old tavern was renamed the Plantation, and the family focused on farming the adjoining lands. After a few years, John Thornton tore down the north and west wings of the building, as they weren't being used. His son Samuel Thornton inherited the property at the age of twenty-two following John's sudden death in 1846. Wanting to be closer to town, Samuel moved his family to Akron in 1857, yet his children continued to occupy the former tavern on and off until 1905, when they moved away and rented it out to other families.

On September 1, 1924, a newspaper article shared information regarding a haunting at the ancient tavern, which was still being used as a private residence. According to the stories that were circulating at the time, an old

A view of the staircase that leads to the attic. *Photo by William G. Krejci.*

peddler had stopped in at the tavern one night when it was still relatively new and under the ownership of George Rex. Like almost every other travel-weary guest who would stretch out in the taproom, stir their grog and stare mistily into the flickering flames of the warming fireplace, so, too, did this aged wandering merchant. He was last seen down in that taproom late one night, and from there, he disappeared without a trace. For more than a century, mysterious noises were heard coming from the attic of the old tavern. This was believed to be the ghost of the missing peddler. It was said that if the crowd in the downstairs taproom grew too loud and boisterous, the peddler's ghost would be heard dragging chains across the attic floor.

In 1925, the old structure was returned to its original purpose when James Milton Thornton, Samuel's son, converted it back into a tavern and named it Ye Old Homestead Inn. The name was slightly altered a year later to The Old Homestead Inn. In late 1938, the business came under new management, and the name of the establishment was changed to White House Tavern. It continued to operate under that name through 1982. The following year, the name was changed to Whitehouse Lounge, which the tavern operated under until the end of the 1988 season. The following year, it reopened as the Upper Deck, which featured a lakeside patio bar and grill—and still does.

Curiously enough, there still appears to be some activity up in the attic of the former Rex's Tavern. When visiting the place in the early spring of

A present-day view of the Upper Deck, taken from the parking lot. *Photo by William G. Krejci.*

2025, I shared what I was writing about with one of the bartenders, and she seemed a little astonished. Apparently, some of the staff say the attic is haunted, even though none of them had ever heard the stories of the peddler's ghost from over one hundred years ago. It was admitted that quite a few of the staff members have heard strange sounds coming from the attic, but they believed it to be the ghost dragging a chair across the floor. They never guessed that it could have been a chain.

Chair or chain—it sounds like something's being dragged around up there.

36

THERE'S A GHOST AT THE DOOR

While I nodded, nearly napping, suddenly there came a tapping,
As of some one gently rapping, rapping at my chamber door.
"'Tis some visitor," I muttered, "tapping at my chamber door—
Only this, and nothing more."
—"The Raven," by Edgar Allan Poe

We conclude this work, simply enough, with a story of a haunted house. There's no biographical background for reference, nor is there a history of the site. This one is just a good old-fashioned ghost story, short and sweet. Once again, very little information was given regarding the house's location, and nothing at all could be learned in relation to the people whose names were provided. Perhaps you, the reader, will discover the truth for yourself should you decide to take a stab at researching this one. In this case, I wish you the best of luck in your endeavor.

Our final story took place in Summit County on January 15, 1925. It was on that day that news broke of a haunting that had troubled the occupant of a rented house so much that he was forced to move out. The house in question was located in the heart of a west side business district in the town of Barberton, about six miles southwest of Akron. Vernon Teagle, the occupant until about a week earlier, claimed that he would close and lock the doors before bed, but they would suddenly fly open during the night. He'd get up to close and lock them once more, but in the morning, he would find them unbolted and wide open. Furthermore, he stated that the noises at

SPOOKS IN HOUSE AT BARBERTON

Slamming of Doors, Deep Groans and Tramping of Feet Heard by Newspaper Reporters

A headline reports on the haunting in Barberton. *From the* Galion Inquirer, *January 15, 1925.*

night had become too much to tolerate, stating that music could be heard in all parts of the house.

Starting on the afternoon of January 13, two days earlier, a pair of reporters from a newspaper in Akron were invited to come and investigate the matter for themselves. They first made a sweep of the house during the daylight hours to look for any available hiding places where a possible prankster might be able to conceal themselves. They found none.

As the sun went down, the activity commenced. The reporters both claimed they heard what sounded like bare feet trampling across the wooden floors throughout the house. The rattling and slamming of doors, as well as the sounds of deep moans and groans, were distinctly heard by both reporters. The noises moved mysteriously, they said, and seemed to always be in a part of the house farthest from where they were. They would run to that part of the house, and as soon as they entered the room the sound was emanating from, it would suddenly stop and then pick up in another room at the other end of the house. This continued for a number of hours until the reporters decided to call it a night.

They returned the following evening, and it was more of the same. The next morning found them both outside the house, comparing notes on all they had witnessed in the course of their investigation. From there, they wrote their experiences down and sent them out on the wire. The story was picked up by multiple newspapers across the country, and overnight, it became something of a national sensation.

Two days later, a very different article appeared in the papers. Joe Kuravik, the owner of the reportedly haunted house in Barberton, put a kibosh on all attempts to solve the mystery of the ghostly activity at his property. Since the release of the first article that reported on the haunting, curiosity seekers had broken into his home numerous times and fairly wrecked the place while attempting to have an experience with the inhabitants from the realm beyond.

More than three hundred people had descended on the house each night since the story broke, and neighbors were complaining that they couldn't sleep, owing to the noise the crowd was making. Barberton police were finally called in to secure the home. Furthermore, Joe Kuravik made it plainly clear that he would "make it hot" for the first person he caught inside his house, ghost or human.

The final statement from the last article on the matter of the haunted house in Barberton read: "Unless police investigate, Barberton's haunted house mystery will remain unsolved."

Guess what?

CONCLUSION

The stories are out there. This is only a small handful of the forgotten ghostly tales that exist right here in our neck of the woods. Just think about how many more tales have yet to be rediscovered, and as you do so, ask yourself this: Have any of these forgotten hauntings occurred in my own home?

Have they?

BIBLIOGRAPHY

Akron (OH) *Beacon Journal*, 1886–2015.

Akron (OH) *Daily Democrat*. "Killed in a Collision with a Water Toboggan." August 15, 1901.

Akron (OH) *Times Democrat*, September 23, 1885.

Ancestry. https://www.ancestry.com.

Ashtabula County Atlas. Sill, Tucker, & Company, 1905.

Ashtabula County Auditor. https://www.auditor.ashtabulacounty.us.

Ashtabula (OH) *Weekly Telegraph*, 1859–75.

Atlas and Directory of Lorain County, Ohio. The American Atlas Company, 1896.

Atlas and Directory of Medina County, Ohio. The American Atlas Company, 1897.

Atlas and Industrial Geography of Summit County, Ohio. The Rectigraph Abstract & Title Company, 1910.

Atlas of Cuyahoga County and the City of Cleveland, Ohio. Geo. F. Cram & Company, 1892.

Atlas of Portage County, Ohio. H.B. Stranahan & Co., 1900.

Atlas of Surveys of Mahoning County, Ohio. A.H. Mueller Co., 1899.

Becker, M.J., and Klauprech & Menzel. *Map of Coshocton County, Ohio*. M.J. Becker, 1850.

Beers, F.W. *Atlas of Jefferson County, Ohio*. F.W. Beers & Co., 1871.

Belmont Chronicle, and Farmers, Mechanics and Manufacturers Advocate. "A Haunted House." May 17, 1894.

Biographical History of Northeastern Ohio: Embracing the Counties of Ashtabula, Geauga, and Lake. The Lewis Publishing Company, 1893.

Bock, George J., Jr. *Atlas of Coshocton County, Ohio*. George J. Bock Jr., 1910.
Brown, James P. *Atlas of the Suburbs of Cleveland, Ohio*. A.H. Mueller & Co., 1898.
Brown, J.P. *Map of Portage Co., Ohio*. Matthews and Taintor Publishers, 1857.
Business Directory for the City of Cleveland. Knight & Parsons, 1853.
Butler, Jos. G., Jr. *History of Youngstown and the Mahoning Valley, Ohio*. Vol. 3. American Historical Society, 1921.
Canfield, J.W., and William Schuchman. *Map of Mahoning County, Ohio: Showing the Original Lots and Farm*. J.W. Canfield, 1860.
Canton (OH) *Repository*, 1818–21.
Chagrin Valley Times (Chagrin Falls, OH). "Century House Destroyed in Blaze." January 15, 2014.
Chapman, Chas. C. *History of Washtenaw County, Michigan*. Chas C. Chapman & Co., 1881.
Chronicle Telegram (Elyria, OH), 1901–59.
Cincinnati (OH) *Daily Inquirer*. "Found Dead." May 7, 1870.
Cincinnati (OH) *Inquirer*. "An Interesting Case." March 2, 1887.
Cincinnati (OH) *Post*, 1922–25.
City Atlas of Cleveland, Ohio: From Official Records, Private Plans and Actual Surveys. G.M. Hopkins, 1881.
Cleveland (OH) *Daily Advertiser*, March 27–October 7, 1837.
Cleveland (OH) *Daily Leader*, January 26, 1866.
Cleveland (OH) *Gazette*, May 31, 1890.
Cleveland (OH) *Herald*. "Valuable Property for Sale." August 1, 1836.
Cleveland Historical. https://www.clevelandhistorical.com.
Cleveland Historic Maps. https://www.arcgis.com/apps/view/index.
Cleveland (OH) *Leader*, 1863–1912.
Cleveland Leader Annual City Directory, 1867–68. Cleveland Leader, 1867.
Cleveland Memory. https://www.clevelandmemory.org.
Cleveland (OH) *Morning Leader*, June 27, 1860.
Cleveland (OH) *Press*, 1892–1925.
Cleveland Public Library. https://www.cpl.org.
Columbus (OH) *Dispatch*, 1897–1910.
Combination Atlas Map of Summit County, Ohio. Tackabury, Mead & Moffett, 1874.
Coshocton (OH) *Daily Age*. "Whiskey Spring the Haunt of Spooks." January 6, 1905.
The County of Richland, Ohio. An Imperial Atlas and Art Folio. Rerick Brothers, 1896.
Cram, George F. *Atlas of Cuyahoga County and the City of Cleveland, Ohio*. Geo. F. Cram & Co., 1892.
Cuyahoga County Auditor. https://www.cuyahogacounty.gov.

Cuyahoga County Recorder. https://www.cuyahoga.ohio.publicsearch.us.
Daily Herald and Gazette (Cleveland, OH), July 25–December 6, 1838.
Daily Jeffersonian (Cambridge, OH). "Ghosts Forced Him to Move." January 15, 1925.
Daily Times (New Philadelphia, OH). "Legend of Whiskey Spring and Headless Cow Recalled." October 17, 1913.
Danner, John. *Old Landmarks of Canton and Stark County, Ohio*. B.F. Bowen, 1904.
Democrat and Standard (Coshocton, OH), February 5, 1904.
Democratic Press (Ravenna, OH), 1871–94.
Duncan, L. Wallace, and Chas. F. Scott. *History of Allen and Woodson Counties, Kansas*. Iola Register, 1901.
Elyria (OH) *Reporter*, 1900–1901.
Elyria (OH) *Republican*. "All About That Ghost." September 5, 1901.
Elyria (OH) *Republican and Working Men's Advocate*, 1835–37.
Encyclopedia of Cleveland History. https://www.case.edu/ech.
Evening Post (Cleveland, OH), 1847–82.
Evening Press (Cleveland, OH), November 9, 1885.
Everts, L.H. *Combination Atlas Map of Medina County, Ohio*. L.H. Everts, 1874.
———. *Combination Atlas Map of Portage County, Ohio*. L.H. Everts, 1874.
———. *Combination Atlas Map of Stark County, Ohio*. L.H. Everts & Co., 1875.
Family Search. https://www.familysearch.org.
Find a Grave. https://www.findagrave.com.
Flynn, Thomas. *Atlas of the Suburbs of Cleveland, Ohio*. A.H. Mueller & Company, 1898.
Galion (OH) *Inquirer*. "Spooks in House at Barberton." January 15, 1925.
Geil, John F. *Map of Lorain County, Ohio*. Matthews and Taintor Publishers, 1857.
———. *Map of Medina County, Ohio*. Matthews and Taintor Publishers, 1857.
Genealogy Bank. https://www.genealogybank.com.
Google Maps. https://www.google.com/maps.
Grant, C.R. *Illustrated Summit County, Ohio*. Akron Map & Atlas Co., 1891.
Hall, Mary Beebe. *Reminiscence of Elyria, Ohio*. The Lorain County Historical Society, 1900.
History of Lorain County, Ohio. Williams Brothers, 1879.
History of Trumbull and Mahoning Counties. H.Z. Williams & Bro., 1882.
Hopkins, Griffith Morgan, Jr., and S.H. Mathews. *Map of Cuyahoga County, Ohio: From Actual Surveys & County Records, Under the Supervision of G.M. Hopkins Jr. C.E.* S.H. Mathews, 1858.

Insurance Maps of Cleveland, Ohio. Vols. 1–3. Sanborn Map & Publishing Co., 1886.

Insurance Maps of Cleveland, Ohio. Vols. 1–2B. Sanborn-Perris Map Co., 1896.

Insurance Maps of Cleveland, Ohio. Vols. 1–11. Sanborn Map & Publishing Co., 1912–13.

Insurance Maps of Cleveland, Ohio. Vols. 1–12. Sanborn Map & Publishing Co., 1886–1918.

Insurance Maps of Cleveland, Ohio. Vols. 4A–5B. Sanborn Map & Publishing Co., 1903.

Johnson, Crisfield. *History of Cuyahoga County, Ohio: In Three Parts, With Portraits and Biographical Sketches of Its Prominent Men and Pioneers*. Greater Cleveland Genealogical Society, 1879.

Kauffman, William J., and Orrin F. Kauffman. *Atlas of Stark County, Ohio*. The Ohio Map and Atlas Co., 1896.

Kenney, Kimberly A. *Canton's Pioneers in Flight*. Arcadia Publishing, 2007.

———. *Canton's West Lawn Cemetery*. Arcadia Publishing, 2004.

Krause, F.L. *Atlas of the City of Cleveland Ohio in One Volume*. A.H. Mueller & Company, 1898.

Lake, D.J. *Atlas of Ashtabula County, Ohio. From Actual Surveys by and Under the Directions of D.J. Lake, C.E.* Titus, Simmons, & Titus, 1874.

———. *Atlas of Coshocton County, Ohio: From Actual Surveys by and Under the Directions of D.J. Lake, C.E.* C.O. Titus, 1872.

———. *Atlas of Cuyahoga County, Ohio: From Actual Surveys by and Under the Directions of D.J. Lake, C.E.* Titus, Simmons & Titus, 1874.

———. *Atlas of Lake and Geauga Counties, Ohio: From Actual Surveys by and Under the Directions of D.J. Lake, C.E.* Titus, Simmons & Titus, 1874.

———. *Atlas of Lorain County, Ohio: From Actual Surveys by and Under the Directions of D.J. Lake, C.E.* Titus, Simmons & Titus, 1874.

———. *Atlas of Mahoning County, Ohio: From Actual Surveys by and Under the Directions of D.J. Lake, C.E.* Titus, Simmons & Titus, 1874.

Lane, Samuel A. *Fifty Years and Over of Akron and Summit County*. Beacon Job Department, 1892.

Large, Moina W. *History of Ashtabula County, Ohio*. Historical Publishing Company, 1924.

Lawrence, C.H., and L.W. Griffin. *Atlas of Lorain County, Ohio*. The Century Printing Co. 1912.

Lehman, John H. *A Standard History of Stark County, Ohio*. The Lewis Publishing Company, 1916.

Library of Congress. https://www.loc.gov.

Lorain County Auditor. https://www.loraincountyauditor.com.
Lorain (OH) *Journal*, August 8, 1941.
Massullo, Brandon. *Haunted Medina County, Ohio*. The History Press, 2022.
Medina County Auditor. https://www.medinacountyauditor.org.
Medina (OH) *Sentinel*, 1917–21.
Monroe Street Cemetery Foundation. https://www.mscf1841.org.
"MyPlace." Cuyahoga County. https://myplace.cuyahogacounty.gov.
Northern Ohio Journal (Painesville, OH), October 2, 1875.
Ohio Democrat (New Philadelphia, OH). "Affidavit of E. Pardee." March 17, 1842.
"Ohio GenWeb." Cuyahoga County. https://usgenwebsites.org/OHCuyahoga.
Ohio Repository (Canton, OH), 1834–53.
Ottawa County Exponent (Oak Harbor, OH), June 14, 1913.
Paul, Hosea. *Map of Summit Co., Ohio*. Matthews & Taintor, 1856.
Perrin, William Henry. *History of Stark County, Ohio.* Baskin & Battey, 1881.
Philadelphia (PA) *Inquirer*. "A Ghost Story." July 27, 1870.
Pittsburgh (PA) *Commercial*, July 28, 1870.
Plain Dealer (Cleveland, OH), 1858–1968.
Plat Book of Cuyahoga County, Ohio. Vols. 1–7. G.M. Hopkins Company, 1920–43.
Plat Book of the City of Akron, Ohio and Vicinity, Including Barberton, Cuyahoga Falls, and Kenmore: From Official Records, Private Plans and Actual Surveys. G.M. Hopkins Co., 1915–21.
Plat Book of the City of Cleveland, Ohio and Suburbs, Complete in Two Volumes: From Official Records, Private Plans and Actual Surveys. G.M. Hopkins Co., 1912–14.
Portage County Democrat (Ravenna, OH), 1868–69.
Portage Sentinel (Ravenna, OH), March 15, 1852.
Record Courier (Ravenna, OH). "Fight with Council Brews as Ritenour Opposes Plan to Repair Hotchkiss Mansion, Park Commission Burning Down Old Hotchkiss House, Quits Park Board in Protest Over Razing of Hotchkiss House, Hotchkiss Fire Lamentable Historian Lowrie Declares." April 5–June 8, 1949.
Repository (Canton, OH), 1885–1906.
Richland County Auditor. https://www.richlandcountyoh.gov/departments/auditor.
Saturday Globe (Utica, NY). "Roasted to Death." July 11, 1891.

Schuchman, William. *New Map of Stark County, Ohio*. Williams Dorr & Co., 1850.
Sidney (OH) *Daily News*. "Asphyxiated by Gas." October 25, 1895.
Smith, Robert Pearsall. *Ashtabula County, Ohio*. Robert Pearsall Smith, 1856.
———. *Map of Geauga and Lake Counties, Ohio*. S.H. Matthews, 1857.
Stark County Democrat (Canton, OH), 1897–1907.
Stark County, Ohio. https://www.starkcountyohio.gov.
Stranahan, H.B. *Atlas of Lake County, Ohio*. H.B. Stranahan & Co., 1898.
———. *Geauga County, Ohio*. H.B. Stranahan & Co., 1900.
———. *Maps of Cuyahoga County Outside of Cleveland*. H.B. Stranahan & Co., 1903.
Strong, Reverend A.H. *The Uncertainty of Life. Sermon Preached with Reverence to the Death of Mary Keokee Monroe, in the First Baptist Church, Cleveland, Sunday, January 28th 1866*. N.p., 1866.
Summit County Beacon (Akron, OH), 1842–92.
Summit Memory. https://www.summitmemory.org.
Times Recorder (Zanesville, OH), June 12, 1905.
Tri-State Alliance (Pioneer, OH). "Smothered by Gas." November 19, 1895.
Trumbull County Archives. https://www.co.trumbull.oh.us.
Van Tassel, David D., and John J. Grabowski, eds. *The Encyclopedia of Cleveland History*. Indiana University Press, in association with Case Western Reserve University and the Western Reserve Historical Society, 1996.
Wayne County Democrat (Wooster, OH), September 4, 1895.
Weekly News (Mansfield, OH). "Thinks the House Is Haunted." March 17, 1892.
Western Reserve Historical Society. https://www.wrhs.org.
Wikipedia. https://www.wikipedia.org.
Williams, William W. *History of Ashtabula County, Ohio*. Williams Brothers, 1878.
Youngstown (OH) *Vindicator*. "Ghost Walks." February 24, 1897.
Ypsilanti (MI) *Commercial*, March 9, 1888.
Zanesville (OH) *Signal*, April 29, 1887.

About the Author

Photo by Christina Johnson.

Author and investigative historian William G. Krejci was born in Cleveland and raised in neighboring Avon Lake. Aside from the multiple book titles to his credit, he's also the owner, operator, and host of Strange & Spooky Cleveland Tours. With an interest in local history, he spends much of his time investigating the origins of ghostly legends and urban lore, and for six years was the resident historian of Cleveland's famed Franklin Castle. Since 2022, he's served on the board of the Monroe Street Cemetery Foundation on Cleveland's West Side. William has been a guest speaker at many historical societies, libraries, bookstores, public venues and civic groups, has appeared on local television and radio, and has been a guest on multiple paranormal-based television programs. In his free time, he enjoys hiking with friends, playing guitar and singing in an Irish band.